A REASON TO HOPE

For All Who Feel...Abandoned, Imprisoned,
and Hunger for...Being Free and Living Their Dream

JEFFREY A. SIEGEL

xulon PRESS

A Reason to Hope
For All Who Feel...Abandoned, Imprisoned, and Hunger for...Being Free and Living Their Dream
by Jeffrey A. Siegel

Printed in the United States of America.

ISBN 9781498451635

While all the legal and prison narratives are true, the names of the principals have been changed to respect their privacy.

www.xulonpress.com

What people are saying about *A Reason to Hope...*

"I first met Jeff Siegel several years ago when he was applying to our D.Min. program at Alliance Seminary. When I heard his story of brokenness and Grace, I was thrilled that he was joining us. This book now puts in print the marvelous miracle of Jeff's life. All who read it will be inspired to trust God to do the miraculous in their lives. Thank you, Jeff, and thank you, Jesus!"

–Dr. Ron Walborn, Dean, Alliance Theological Seminary

"Jeff's story is one of those rare commodities where we learn about the true meaning of being a born again Christian. Jeff has bared his heart and soul writing about his walk with Jesus. He faced strong opposition as a Jewish Believer early in his walk and faced a more difficult task, prison and separation from his family, after a boy died in his church. The redemptive love of our Messiah is great and never fails. Jeff is a living testament to Jesus' faithfulness and grace. If I were to add a subtitle to the story I would pen, "Humility, How Hard Is That?" Humility and facing the truth of God in your life is hard. Jeff's story will walk you through something that usually only people of the Bible go through. Jeff is now one of our great Evangelists and tells all of us A *Reason to Hope.*"

–Jeff Goldberg, MPA, author of *Blind Authority*

"I am so overwhelmed with your manuscript. I have not read a book in all my years that has elicited such amazement as far as content, purpose, and details. I actually was carried into the emotions and situations you describe. This is such a powerhouse testimony of God's love for His creation in that if we seek, God will reveal. God's blessings on you as you carry this long time endeavor to its end."

–Pat Mielke, Anderson, SC

"I have received such a blessing from reading your manuscript. This is a great book. It touched my heart and captured my attention from the first page. I found myself so engrossed in your life story, to the point I couldn't put the manuscript down. I could feel the cry of your heart, and God's response. This book is a beautiful picture of God's amazing grace. Thank you for allowing me to read it."

–Carol Vass, Greenville, SC

"As you read of Jeff's great sorrow, hopelessness and despair, you will follow his journey from prison to repentance, reconciliation and eventual restoration. This story speaks about God's great love, His mercy, forgiveness, and His ability to rescue and restore the brokenhearted, resulting in ultimate fulfillment in life."

–Winston Severn Owner, All Pro Sports, Agoura Hills, CA
Former USA International Cricket Player

"Knowing Jeff for over 50 years, this book tells well the story of his success, finding truth, tragedies of pride—power and following others, punishment (jail), deliverance, grace, forgiveness, and power of God. Determination, faith, hard work, hope, relationships, and the grace of God have been the new tools given to Jeff replacing his youthful pride, stubbornness, and most of all, sin against God and man. I cried and laughed many times reading this book which is really the story of God's hand on one man, as well as God's hand and will for each of us. I left this book both encouraged and challenged to grow in my own faith, move beyond my weaknesses and fears, while allowing God to do his work though me."

–**Neal Siegel**, President/ Co-founder Tri-Media Marketing,
Men's Ministry at Vineyard Christian Church, Northbrook, IL

"In *A Reason to Hope*, we see God turn a triple play of redemption in the life of Jeff Siegel. First, Jeff finds salvation through the influence of his friends. Secondly, he finds his literal freedom after doctrinal error contributed to the death of a child and Jeff's incarceration. Thirdly, God gives Jeff a fulfilling future by calling him to start a world-wide ministry using baseball as a platform to share the gospel. It is an inspiring story which I expect will give many a reason to hope."

–**Stephen E. Garner,** Murphy & Garner, LLC

"Reading and reviewing scores of books each year, I am rarely moved by the raw emotion and powerful demonstration of man's failure and God's unlimited mercy and grace. Jeff's testimony of repentance, forgiveness, grace, and victory will bring tears, joy, and hope to all who read it. It's a story impossible to put down until you have read it all."

–**Dr. Larry Keefauver**, Bestselling author and International Teacher

A Reason to Hope

For All Who Feel...
Abandoned, Imprisoned, & Hunger for...
Being Free & Living Their Dreams

Jeff Siegel

Dedication

To my wife, Terri...

I want to take this moment to express the depth of my love and respect for you. You have been an angel to me for more than thirty-six years. I am thankful for your love for our Savior, your daily love to me and our family. I want to thank our Lord who has given us His mercy and grace to journey on together in His ministry of hope.

Acknowledgments

Championships are won through teamwork. My friend, Brian Doyle, who played on the Yankees 1978 World Series Championship team, once said to me that no one person wins a championship alone. It takes a team.

I am grateful for the people the Lord brought into my life to make this book possible. There is no way I could have done this on my own. I would have never considered taking on such a task without the help of good people in my life.

I want to thank Pastor Dale Crawshaw, who is one of the most selfless and encouraging people I ever met. He came to me with the idea of writing this book in the year 2000. I want to thank Mark Burns and Huey Freeman for helping me get started with the book. Huey, thanks for your writing tips. To Carl and Wanda King, who are dear friends, Wanda, thanks for your help with editing. Many thanks to Dr. Larry Keefauver, who coached and helped me to fine-tune this book.

Thank you to Brian Doyle, my accountability partner, for your friendship all these years. Many thanks to Jeff Goldberg, Neal Siegel, Win Severn, Steven Garner, Carol Vass, Marty Clary, and Pat Mielke for your encouragement and support. I want to thank the Board of Directors of Global Baseball for giving me the time to write this book. To Toby and

Rita Kahr, my parents in the Lord and my mentors. To my brothers, Rick and Bruce, thanks for being supportive all these years.

My wife, Terri, is the most beautiful person I have ever known. She is gracious, humble, and wise. We have had a life of purpose and joy all of these years together. She stuck with me during our dark night. As a result, our children have grown up to become three honorable and accomplished adults. We are so proud of Melissa, Joseph, and Benjamin. God's greatest kindness to us is our children. May they all surpass anything that Terri and I will ever accomplish in our lifetime.

There was a moment in my life when I was tempted to give up. It seemed like all hope was gone. Terri, my children, and godly friends never let go of me. They prayed because they saw past my failure and what the future could be if I would have a change of heart and turn to the Lord.

Thankfully, I did and the story you are about to read is true. The Lord was not done with me. He reached down and snatched me from Satan's grip. He had a plan. Thank God for friends and family who prayed for me and continue to do so every day.

Foreword

WOW! That was the first reaction after I read "A Reason to Hope." "WOW" is also what I said the day I met Jeff the first time. I have known Jeff for over twenty years. We have been prayer partners and accountability partners for that long. He was so fascinating to me being a Messianic Jew or "Completed Jew." I have had such a love for Israel and the children of Abraham, Isaac, and Jacob since the day that I was saved by the grace of God. Jeff is a brother in Christ that is REAL. There are no false faces that he hides behind. He is not a man that changes colors depending on the audience or circumstance. He is a true man of God that has constantly shown his faithfulness to our Lord and Savior, Jesus Christ.

At the very beginning of our relationship, Jeff was one of my trained professional baseball instructors. He learned quickly and rose to the top in a very short period of time. His first chapel service, during the Doyle School of Baseball, he saw God save over forty students and adults. God showed Jeff a glimpse of what he was going to do for His Kingdom.

Jeff has shown me what a loving husband and father should be. No matter the situation or turmoil, his love for his family stays constant. He has shown me what a Christian businessman should be. He also has shown me what a Christian leader should be. I am not saying that Jeff is perfect. What I am saying is that Jeff's imperfections are out in front, never covered up or hidden. More importantly, he hears the Holy Spirit and obeys when he hears. That means he corrects that which is broken. This is what each and every one of us should do as followers of Jesus.

As you read "A Reason to Hope," you will definitely understand why Jeff chose the title. I have watched this man live by faith. He has not written this book to show anything but that...there is a reason to hope. He has been counted as dead by his earthly father, he has been rejected by his father-in-law and mother-in-law. He has been and still is one of the hardest workers that I have ever known. You will read of his many diversified job experiences. He has been in prison and has been abased more than anyone that I have known. Through all of the adversities, Jeff sought and pursued Jesus, knowing that He has ordered his steps.

On the other hand, God has allowed him to stand before kings, diplomats, and various national government ministers. Jeff has shared the Good News of Jesus Christ to the poorest in the world and to the richest in the world. He has shared the Gospel of Jesus Christ to a poor child and to a ruler's grown son, both becoming born again. I know this because he would call and we would pray about each and every place that God would have him go. I also know this because God has blessed me to be part of Global Baseball's ministry and I have lived with, ministered with, and witnessed this man's faith.

God had Jeff pioneer Global Youth Baseball Federation, Inc. and to this day I cannot imagine how he has accomplished so much for God. God had Jeff doing everything, that a ministry that travels the world does, all by himself. Through God's timing, others have come to be full-time Global Baseball Pros. Through this transition, Jeff has shown how to lift younger men on his shoulders so that God can use these young men in sports ministry around the world. These men are learning through Jeff's experience and leadership by the grace of God, His mercy, and His provision in every area of their lives.

I personally witnessed this man of God sleep in the nicest room and on a mattress on the floor. I have seen him abased and I have seen him abound. Like Paul, Jeff has not wavered in his faith and faithfulness to proclaim the goodness of God. There is one thing that completes this foreword for "A Reason to Hope." Jeff Siegel is a man that does not make decisions unless he hears from the Holy Spirit. Then he seeks brothers and sisters to pray with him in order to secure the Lord's full counsel and blessing.

Being kicked out of his family, participating in a deceiving cult, sentenced to prison, tossed out of great provision into complete faith in the Provider, this book will give you a reason to hope. It will give you a real live person who has experienced and demonstrated his love for God and God's love for him. This same hope and love is also there for you. All you have to do is really want it. "A Reason to Hope" is the story of Jeff Siegel being "all in." *Are you?*

–**Rev. Brian Doyle**
Executive VP of Global Baseball,
Christian and Baseball Curriculum Writer
NY Yankees 1978 World Series Champion
and Leading Hitter

TABLE OF CONTENTS

Jeff shares his Jewish roots from immigrant grandparents to a dysfunctional family. His pride in his Jewish heritage shines through memories of the people who shaped and influenced his early childhood.

Jeff learns what it means to be a Jew through his friendship with the cantor of his synagogue, who gave him Bar Mitzvah lessons and who was also offered a professional baseball contract. He learns character and commitment to the Jewish people through the lives of famous Jewish baseball players like Sandy Koufax and Kenny Holtzman.

Puberty hits as Jeff balances his love for baseball and his new-found love for girls. He weathers high school during the Vietnam War years and feels the sting of anti-Semitism.

Jeff traces his baseball history. He moves into his university years cool and cocky, making a name for himself on the baseball field. Players in his life's story begin to assemble. The stage is set.

God begins to knock at Jeff's heart door. Questions surface: *Does God have a plan for my life? Why was I born anyway?* Jeff initiates his search to understand just who this Jesus is. At the same time he suffers a physical setback to his baseball career.

Seemingly on top of the world, Jeff is filled with great turmoil. He remembers his promise to God and sets out to fulfill it. His resulting cry is, "God, can I have a burning bush experience like Moses? Is Jesus the promised Jewish Messiah?"

Jeff discovers the trials and tribulations of a Jew who accepts Yeshua as the Messiah. Rejection comes from his family and his Jewish friends. Jeff finds solace in a Christian Bible study that took place once a week in his Jewish fraternity house.

Influenced by those who were instrumental in leading him to faith in Jesus, Jeff follows the spiritual leaders in his life as they move away from traditional Christian paths. His personal life begins to come into focus for Jeff as he meets Terri, his future wife. Neither Jeff's Jewish family nor Terri's parents support their marriage.

Terri and Jeff begin their new life together. A new church begins. Jeff becomes an elder and new responsibilities come. Feeling that he is closely following God, Jeff is blind to the false doctrine and he wholeheartedly accepts and cannot imagine the dire consequences for him and his family.

Activities within the Fellowship become more and more fanatical. Despite wise counsel from outsiders and people who began to leave the group, Jeff continues to follow the spiritual leadership to whom he had submitted himself. Life as he knows it unravels. Cool, cocky, confident Jeff hits bottom—felony charges.

Jeff faces the charges against him relating to the death of a young boy in his congregation. As he begins to go through the indictment process, he comes to the full realization of his sins. Jeff stands up for the dead boy's mother, which leads to her release. Even though he has begged Terri to leave him, she stands by him and is relieved when he can fully face up to what has happened.

Jeff enters the prison system. The Lord begins dealing with him as he faces the challenges of prison life. His encounters with sexual deviants, drug users, and prison gangs lead to threats against his life. But the Lord providentially saves him from the situations that arise, even using baseball as a means, and miraculously prepares him for his release from prison.

Jeff returns to North Carolina to be with his family. His longtime mentor, Toby Kahr, helps Jeff get a job. He moves through several jobs in an effort to support his family and to make up for time lost. He receives various words of encouragement as people share with him words of knowledge from the Lord. God's finger seems to point him toward ministry, but Jeff sees his sin as a roadblock.

Jeff begins a new life and becomes employed by ServiceMaster and begins to climb the management ladder. He moves south and learns southern culture and cuisine. His children accept Christ and his life begins to be restored. The Lord uses Jeff even as he works in management.

As Jeff becomes involved with an adult baseball league at the age of thirty-eight, he comes to know the Doyle family and becomes a professional instructor. He travels extensively with Doyle Baseball schools while still employed with ServiceMaster. Traveling to Germany, to do free baseball programs for young adults, Jeff is deeply moved at the history of his people there, even as he comes face-to-face with modern-day anti-Semitism.

The Lord brings interesting contacts into Jeff's life as his career advances. As he moves his family because of business, the Lord brings special people and ministries into his life.

Prologue

My Damascus Road

In December 1987, Robert Cline, who, was the overseer of five churches made a trip to Spokane, where I was the elder in charge. A ten-year-old boy named Alan Peters came forward with his parents in a service to receive prayer from the leaders. This young boy had symptoms of a serious illness. He was eating constantly and urinating very often and did not feel well. Instead of addressing the medical symptoms, Robert began questioning the boy and his parents about his personal life. His parents said the boy was masturbating with his friends. Robert said he was an evil little boy and that God was judging him. That was why he was sick, and he would have to repent.

After the service all the elders, Robert and I went to the boy's home with his parents. Robert told them that he thought his sickness was a result of the child's sin. I remember Robert quoting to me Bible verses about young evil kings in the Hebrew Scriptures. He compared Alan to one of these kings.

A man named John, who belonged to the congregation, was a diabetic. He told us he believed Alan's symptoms indicated he may have diabetes.

My wife, Terri, looked up the symptoms in a medical manual and said, "Jeff, I think he has diabetes. He needs to go to the doctor."

I had been preaching that the Lord could heal; consequently, there was a lot of pressure coming from my preaching not to see a doctor and believe that the Lord would heal if you had the faith. While we were praying for the boy, he was getting sicker and sicker. His father, George Peters, called our home one night and told Robert that he was greatly concerned for Alan, who was really sick. His father was greatly concerned that his son could die. Robert and his wife were staying at our home at the time and he came to our room to answer George's phone call. Terri and I heard Robert say to Alan's father, "Your son is going to live. He's not going to die." George really looked up to Robert and wanted to see his son healed by God.

It was a terrible scene. George, wanting to prove his faith to Robert, me, and all the leaders of our church, did not call an ambulance. The next morning, we received a phone call at home. George, the boy's father, said Alan wasn't breathing. It was early Sunday morning and we were getting ready for church when we received the call. All the leaders went to the Peters' home, about six or seven of us. Alan had died.

The death of Alan Peters occurred December 20, 1987.
The boy was lying lifeless on his parents' bed.

The Peters called a funeral home; then the funeral home called the coroner who called the police. When that boy died, something within me died. I had believed that the teaching I heard from Robert was true.

An investigation took place. There was an autopsy. The conclusion was that Alan had died because of untreated diabetes. This was considered gross negligence. It was explained to us that there was going to be an investigation into the negligence. We had progressed from being a fellowship filled with zealous young people who thought they were following the Lord to following a man and had become a full-fledged cult. Now a child had died. I was on the verge of a total meltdown—physical, emotional, mental, and spiritual.

As a result, Terri, and I with our three children moved back to Champaign, IL. Soon after the move, I received a call from Spokane and was told that there were charges against me. I had to attend an arraignment hearing. It was at the hearing that I was told the charges against me could carry up to six years in prison. The judge told me to get a lawyer.

Four of us were charged in the death of the boy—his mother and father, Robert Cline, and I. The other leaders who had been involved in the group had been let off the hook in exchange for providing information on the group.

I looked in the yellow pages and found a lawyer named Alan Gauper. He told me he would talk with the prosecutor and find out what he was planning to do. "What really makes this bad," the lawyer said, "is that it is one thing for a child to die from a lack of medical attention, but another to spank a child who is dying." While I had not been directly involved with spanking the boy, the lawyer said I would be viewed as part of that incident.

"If the prosecutor wants to take this case to the limit," said my lawyer, a former prosecutor himself, "he will use every trick he can to inflame the jury. The jury can be swept along in a wave of emotion." I was afraid. I realized that I could go to prison for a long time.

I also realized that the mom, Janice Peters, was totally innocent as she was trying to tell George and Robert that she was uncomfortable with the whole situation. I felt bad for Janice; she did not participate in anything wrong. The mother just wanted her son to live.

I said to Terri, "I'm not innocent." She said, "I knew that all along. You had a responsibility to get that boy to the doctor. You were a contributing factor in Alan's death."

A Guilty Plea and Prison

"I agree," I said. "I was wrong. I must go with my lawyer, see the prosecuting attorney, and be honest, and plead guilty."

I was also concerned for Janice Peters, and I hoped that the prosecutor would let her go if he knew that she was dominated and could not get her child to the doctor. As a result of my testimony to the prosecutor, the charges were dropped against the boy's mother before her trial was to begin.

I was facing a ninety-day sentence for criminal mistreatment, according to the standard sentencing guidelines in the death of the boy, and an additional year for assault in the spanking of a young woman. My lawyer entered a plea of guilty for me on Wednesday, October 5, 1988, for the charges of felony second-degree criminal mistreatment and misdemeanor assault.

On October 17, 1988, I testified that George Peters was free to take his son to the hospital, even though our cult preached against conventional medicine. My testimony was not intended to hurt George Peters or help him, just to tell the truth, as I understood it.

George Peters' defense was that the church leaders had so much control over him that he could not have obtained medical help for his son. Mr. Peters was found guilty of first-degree manslaughter and sentenced to forty-one months. The judge in the case said to Mr. Peters, "You are ultimately responsible for your son's care." The judge sentenced Robert

Cline to thirty-six months in prison for the charges of felony second-degree criminal mistreatment.

On November 14, 1988, I went before the judge and the prosecutor made his recommendation of ninety days. The judge did not agree with him. He said, "Why is it that it takes a tragedy to realize that what they have been doing is wrong? Medicine has been given to us by God as much as the power of prayer." He also said that he had an obligation to send a message to anyone who might be interested in starting a religious cult.

I was sentenced to twenty-four months for the charge of criminal mistreatment and six months concurrent for the spanking of a member of the Fellowship.

He told me that I would be eligible to go home after sixteen months. My wife, Terri, was shocked and cried about the length of time involved.

On February 14, 1989, I reported to the county jail in Spokane. I gave up my clothes and all personal belongings and was given inmate clothes. I was put in a cell all by myself, the door slammed shut!

I was an absolutely broken man and on my way to my prison cell!

Chapter 1:

The Way of My Fathers

What led to my journey to prison? Let's start at the beginning...

My parents, Sheldon Siegel and Shirley Nemerow, met each other through two friends who went to school with them. My mom went to Von Steuben High School in Chicago, and my father went to Roosevelt High. The schools were a few miles apart from each other. My dad's friend, Jerry was dating a girl named Cybil. Cybil, a friend of my mom, asked Jerry to have one of his friends take my mom out and they would double date.

My dad's teenage and early adult photographs indicate that he was very handsome. My mom was a beautiful, popular young woman with a bubbly personality who excelled as a student. She stood about five-feet tall, with dark wavy hair, deep dark brown eyes, and olive skin. On their first date they went out for dinner, hit it off right away, and continued to date. They liked to go to high school dances together and even went to my father's senior prom.

My mom's mother was named Bernice Nemerow, and she had been married three times. First, Bernice married a butcher named Joseph

Nemerow. He was a soft-spoken immigrant from Kiev, Ukraine, who had a passion for playing cards. This was my mom's dad. He would go away for nights on end like a binge drinker and lose a lot of money playing cards. Joseph had a very friendly personality and made good money in his own butcher shop on the west side of Chicago. But, as a result of the gambling addiction, he lost all of his earnings and this hurt my bubby (the Jewish word for grandmother). After twenty years of marriage, Bernice divorced Joseph, leaving her with three children and no income.

My bubby had to go on public assistance and moved with her three children to Albany Park on Lawndale Avenue. Bernice was married ten years later to a wealthy businessman, an older man named Louis Dancer. He bought a beautiful home on Spaulding Avenue in Hollywood Park. My mom was about fourteen. After living without a dad for several years, my mother appreciated that Mr. Dancer treated her in a very kind manner. He died about two years later.

My bubby, Bernice, married again, this time to an Orthodox Jew named Paul Dermer. He was not a very nice man, and this marriage did not last very long. He had his own home and wanted Bernice to sell her home. My mom and her brothers did not like him and stood in the way of the sale of the home on Spaulding Avenue where my mom, now seventeen years old, was living alone.

After my bubby's divorce from Paul Dermer, she moved back in with my mom on Spaulding Avenue. My bubby began to take in boarders to make some money. She took in a lady named Annie, who had mental problems and was very promiscuous. My mom felt that with multiple boarders living in her home her life was always being invaded. She wanted her mother to get a job so that they could have a life of their own. My bubby did not listen to her, and my mom could not take much more. She was embarrassed by her family situation and terrified by the thought of her friends finding out about Annie. About this time, she met Sheldon Siegel.

My father was an only child and my grandfather, Jack Siegel, had a dream of my father becoming a lawyer. My grandpa explained to me that they only had one child because they were concerned they would not have enough money to support more than one child during the Great Depression. My grandpa an immigrant from Romania and wanted his son to accomplish more than he could. This was the Jewish way in those days—life in their new promised land, the United States.

Jack Siegel came to the United States from Romania with his eighteen-year-old sister Blanche around 1914. He was just sixteen years old. His father sent the children to America first because that was all they could afford. His parents hoped to follow as soon as they could earn their own passage, but a few years later his mother and his father died in Romania. An immigration official changed my grandfather's last name, Segal, to Siegel at Ellis Island.

My dad and mom soon decided to marry. She was seventeen and my dad was nineteen. My mom was just out of high school and my dad was a sophomore at DePaul University. My grandfather objected strongly. My dad did not listen to my grandpa and married my mom anyway. My grandpa never took his frustration with my dad out on my mom. He accepted my mom and treated her respectfully showing her the love she never got growing up. My mom called him Dad, and he showed her the love she never got from her own father. This was the way of my father's parents, very loving people.

My grandfather, however, still nursed the dream of my father being a lawyer. While my dad was at DePaul, my mother discovered she was pregnant with me. He was working part time at a downtown shoe store called Kitty Kelly. He was doing well in school, but had no desire to become a lawyer. So, when he was offered the position of assistant store manager, he suddenly quit school.

My dad was a very hardworking man, but he did not always follow through with important things. My grandpa offered to help with free housing and money for school, but my dad did not accept his generosity and never completed his education. Perhaps he felt pressured to do something that was not in his personal makeup. My dad was very intelligent; he could have completed college and found a profession that better suited his personality. Maybe this would have been a career in management. Perhaps he could have gone back to school a few years later in a field that he enjoyed. But he didn't and my grandpa, coming from the old country, did not know how to mentor and encourage my dad in a direction that would have been better for him.

Decades later, my grandfather told me that there were two things my father did that he could never forgive. I thought maybe he had killed someone or something like that. It turned out that it was that he did not finish school and he married my mom. My grandpa did not want my dad to marry my mom because he thought they were too young and he believed she would stand in the way of his plans for his son. I believe that if my father had finished his bachelor's degree and pursued additional education for the benefit of his family, all would have been forgiven by my grandparents.

Years later, my mother underwent several nervous breakdowns and hospitalizations. You had to wonder if her early childhood environment played a role in her situation. It seemed to me, after I was told about her unusual upbringing, that there was a correlation. Perhaps my grandpa Jack had some wisdom when he advised my dad against marrying my mom at such a young age, especially because of her turbulent upbringing.

**Unforgiveness damages the one offended, the offender,
and those closely relating to both—family and friends.
It also negatively impacts children and children's children
for generations.**

I Enter the Family...

When I came along, my parents were living on the bottom floor of my grandparents' two-flat on North Drake Avenue in Albany Park, Chicago, about one block from their grocery store. Albany Park was a neighborhood consisting of mostly apartment buildings and small shops and was predominantly Jewish, with many immigrants from Russia and Eastern Europe. From the late 1940s through the 1960s, Jews established residences in the northern part of Chicago and in the suburbs to its north including Skokie, Wilmette, Glencoe, Highland Park, Evanston, and Park Forest to the south and Oak Park to the west. By the mid-sixties 80 percent of the Jewish population of the Chicago area were living in the northern communities from Albany Park to the suburb of Wilmette. In the seventies, 70 percent of the population of West Rogers Park and suburban Skokie were Jewish.

I was the first grandchild and spent a lot of time with my grandparents. When I was five years old, we moved just one block away to a flat on Central Park Avenue, an arterial street one block from the grocery store. By this time my two brothers, Ricky and Bruce, were born, and we had outgrown the two-flat on Drake.

No matter what our financial circumstances were, our grandparents were always there for us. Since we lived near their grocery store, our cupboard was never bare. Despite the initial disapproval of my parent's marriage, there remained closeness between my parents and my dad's parents.

In fact, they became very close to my mom, who to this day thinks of them as her own parents and as saints. They never held the marriage against my mom, just against my dad.

A Burning Desire to Play Baseball

My grandfather, however, was unable to understand why my dad never wanted to be a lawyer. In fact, my dad had a burning desire to be a major league baseball player. But instead of encouraging my father to follow his path, he had squelched this ambition a few years earlier. My grandfather was an immigrant from the old country who did not believe a Jewish boy should earn a living on a baseball field. My grandparents had a different idea about the American dream. To them, and many Jewish parents in those days, the American dream could only be fulfilled in one way—through education. My dad resented that my grandpa did not take interest in his love for baseball and never showed up to see him play. He was always busy working in the grocery store.

When my dad finished high school, he had a tryout with the Cincinnati Reds. In those days, professional teams had tryout camps for promising players. He was encouraged by the scouts at the tryout, but my grandfather strongly discouraged him from pursuing a baseball career. My dad was a very fast runner with a strong arm who hit line drives. I watched him play center field and saw him run, hit, and throw. I was always one of the fastest on my university baseball team, but I could never beat my dad in a race. That is a clue as to how fast my dad was.

Living with Grandparents

In third grade, I lived with my grandparents for about half a year. This is because my father got a promotion and transfer to work for Marshall Field and Company at the Old Orchard Store in Skokie, Illinois. We moved to East Rodgers Park on West Farwell Avenue in Chicago. I needed to finish the third grade at my old school as I was in a special program that placed me ahead one half year, so I moved in with my grandparents.

My Grandpa Jack Siegel was a little man about 5'4" and my Grandma Sophie about 4'11". She had come to the United States from Warsaw, Poland, in 1914, at the age of twelve. My grandmother had auburn hair, with dark blue eyes, almost navy blue. When my grandpa came to the States, he took employment tailoring suits. Even though he later went into the grocery business, he often came home in a double-breasted suit and wore a cap with a feather in it. When my grandpa came to my baseball games in high school, I loved putting his hat on my head and mine on his. Jack and Sophie worked side by side in the little grocery store. They looked like characters from the movie, *Fiddler on the Roof.*

My grandfather shaped a lot of my thinking, as he was a good businessman. My grandpa, who was like a second father, would give me a lot of advice about work ethic. He would go to work in the grocery store at about 5:30 in the morning. My grandmother would join him at about 10:00 a.m. Sometimes he would go back into the storage room and take a nap after she arrived. He spoke to me about financial management and the misuse of credit cards.

My grandma could cook. I am telling you Jewish moms and grandmas can cook. When a Jewish grandma tells you that you are looking skinny, don't say a thing because a full-course meal is on the way. This event can begin with chicken soup with matzo balls followed by a full course of paprika chicken, potatoes, and kasha. Jewish food is the best. Yes, there will be Jewish food in heaven. If you dispute this, you can come over to my home any time, and my wife Terri can cook you a good Jewish meal. My grandma, Sophie, and mom took my dear, gentile wife, Terri, and taught her how to cook Jewish.

Have you ever had chicken soup? We call it kosher penicillin as it has been claimed to cure the common cold. When I was sick as a kid and had a few bowls of homemade chicken soup, I was on the road to recovery. I remember watching my mom make chicken soup and asking her if I could try and make a pot under her supervision and I did a pretty good job.

Growing up, going with my grandparents to the local Jewish deli in Chicago was an event for me. The city of Chicago still has many ethnic neighborhoods where you can walk into a Jewish, an Italian, a Romanian or a Hungarian deli and just take in the smells. I'm telling you, it's a prelude of heaven.

During the time I lived with my grandparents, I would go to their house and wait for them to finish their work at the grocery store. Sometimes out of curiosity, I would go through my grandfather's belongings and one day found his silver dollar collection. It was quite large and there were some very old ones. I would steal some of the silver dollars and use them to go to the movie theater on Saturdays to see the Three Stooges. I am not sure if my grandpa ever knew that I did this and was not sure if he noticed the depletion of his collection. I also found in my grandpa's dresser a gun with bullets in it, and I began to take the bullets in and out of the gun. I was curious. I loved taking things apart—vacuums, appliances, etc. There was only one problem; they never got put back together.

My grandpa was a quiet, humble man, but he was a devoted family man. He would always help his relatives when they were in need. I remember him putting wads of money into an envelope. When we had our Siegel Family Club meetings, if he knew a relative was in financial need, he would greet him at the door and quietly slip the envelope into his suit pocket. He did that in such a way that this person would never be embarrassed. He remembered what it was like in the old country and all the hardships he had suffered. My grandpa was always there with a generous heart to help people. His life reminded me of this truth:

> *I was young and now I am old,*
> *yet I have never seen the righteous forsaken*
> *or their children begging bread.*
> *They are always generous and lend freely;*
> *their children will be blessed.*
> (Psalm 37:25-26 NIV)

My grandparents were part of an incredible generation of people. My grandpa Jack died in 1986 after living eighty-eight years. My grandma, Sophie, lived until she was about eighty-eight also. My bubby, Bernice Nemerow, died in 1977 at seventy-seven years of age. My bubby developed mental illness later in life. I am sure that it was from all the scars of her being involved in two failed marriages and another husband dying only after a couple of years of her only good marriage.

My other grandfather, Joseph Nemerow, was born in Kiev, Ukraine, in 1893. His last name was also changed at Ellis Island, from Nemerovsky. I first learned that my grandfather had a different name in the old country when I visited Kiev in 2007. My Ukrainian host told me my grandfather's name would have been Nemerovsky. I later confirmed this with my mother. In May of 2008, I went to Kiev again and my friends showed me on a Ukrainian map that there is a city called Nemerov. Joseph's family probably originated from this city and then moved to Kiev not all that far away. My maternal grandfather Joseph Nemerow died of pancreatic cancer in 1948, at the age of fifty-five, about seven years before I was born. On the eighth day after my birth, at my briss (circumcision), I was given my Hebrew name, Yoseph (Joseph) Aaron Siegel, in honor of him. Because I was born outside of the Promised Land, I was given a second name, a legal American name, Jeffrey Allen Siegel. If I had been born is Israel, I would be called by my Hebrew name.

My Mom—Starved for Love

My mom had two older brothers, Norman and Jerome. Uncle Jerry, twelve years older, was like a father figure to my mom and she was very proud of him. He was tall for our family, about six feet tall, with dark, wavy hair and a mustache—a handsome man with excellent manners. When he was in the military, he studied at Harvard University and later became an eye doctor.

My mother was a kind, generous person, who always had her family's best interest in mind. She would do anything for her children. But my mother was an insecure woman, who was starved for love during her marriage to my father. My father, being an only child, did not know how to share his life with my mom. At times, he could be very harsh and did not show proper appreciation for her. My dad could have a temper and this was just the tip of the iceberg. He could also be a very stubborn and unreasonable person.

My mom was a great cook and I was the recipient of many of her delightful Jewish recipes. One day, my mom made a very delicious meal for my dad. They got into an argument, and my dad threw his meal on the floor at my mom's feet. I was tempted to go after my dad, but something inside said, *That is your dad; walk away*. He never knew what I was thinking at the time, and I did not say anything to him about the incident until many years later. The way my dad's father treated my grandmother was entirely different. I rarely heard my grandparents argue. He loved her, respected her, and sang to her. They would sing to each other "I'll Be Loving You Always."

A good man leaves an inheritance for his children's children (Proverbs 13:22)

What will that inheritance be?

My dad's behavior caused me to disrespect him and created a rift between us. Even though I still loved my dad, it hurt me to see my father and mother argue. Just as I got to high school, which was a difficult time in many ways, it seemed that they were arguing all the time, especially over money and how to pay all the bills. With three boys in the house at the time, my father's paycheck as a manager for a department store was stretched to the max. My dad was also a three-pack-a-day smoker. We didn't know anything about second-hand smoke in those days, but we were inhaling tons of it just the same. I hated to inhale my dad's cigarette smoke and wished he would stop.

At that time, there was a television show called "The Honeymooners" with Jackie Gleason, Jayne Meadows, and Art Carney. My dad really loved that show. Here was this heavyset guy, named Ralph Kramden, a bus driver, and his wife, Alice. Ralph was always telling Alice that he was king of the castle, always fighting for her respect and admiration. My dad had the identical mentality, that he was the king. Unfortunately, he didn't treat my mom like a queen. For me to grow up seeing that really hurt me. When my parents argued, I wished that I could run away from home. The only time I seemed to escape the void and depression I felt inside was when I was on the baseball field, which lifted my spirit in so many ways.

The problems in my family often affected my feelings; but they didn't define my identity or future.

Not long after my mom and my dad celebrated their twenty-fifth wedding anniversary, my mom divorced my dad. Though she had been patient with him for many years, she disrespected him for his stubbornness, harshness, and unwillingness to change, as well as for throwing away his education. The divorce broke his heart; he was never the same. My dad became a reclusive person from that time on. After the divorce, he did not make an effort to spend time with us. We had to do the initiating to get some time with him.

My mom divorced my dad; yet, she still loved him until the day he died. My mom remarried a dear Jewish man named Jack Cohen, and they resided in Pembroke Pines, Florida. Jack was a humble Jewish man and treated my mom like royalty. He helped take her to holistic doctors and get her off of sleeping pills. With a healthy vitamin regimen, my mom had not had any problems with mental illness for many years.

Jeff, age 4

Jeff's dad, Sheldon, age 16

**Jeff's parents, Sheldon and Shirley
and grandparents, Jack and Sophie**

Grandparents-Jack and Sophie Siegel

**Jeff's grandpa, Jack Siegel,
and great grandfather in Romania**

Chapter 2:

Bar Mitzvah and Baseball

A t nine years old, we moved to East Rogers Park on West Farwell Avenue, a real nice area just off Sheridan Road, in an apartment complex with six families. We lived one and a half blocks from the beach on Lake Michigan—swimming, outdoor handball courts, incredible scenery, and pretty girls in bikinis. It was a fun place to grow up. Loyola Park was also a few blocks away with a baseball diamond. We had many pickup games with some pretty good neighborhood ballplayers.

My lifelong friend, Gary Schulman, was a soft-spoken guy who loved baseball and hockey. We gave him the nickname, Schlitz. Gary lived a few blocks from Loyola Park on Estes Avenue, as did friends Neal Siegel on Greenleaf Avenue and Gary Steinberg. From the time I met him, Gary Schulman loved going to the Chicago Cubs baseball games. Gary just wanted to find a way to hang out at Cubs Park, so he became a vendor selling beer and other items.

Gary was quite a likeable guy and he made friends with Chicago Cubs Pitcher, Ferguson Jenkins. Fergie was the Cubs' number one pitcher at the time and is now a Hall of Famer. During the Cubs' playing season, we would rent an indoor skating rink called Rainbow Arena with our friends.

We would divide the cost between about twenty guys, choose sides, and play hockey games for about two hours. Would you believe that Fergie was also a great hockey player as he grew up in Canada? Gary invited him on his day off and he actually came and played. He made Gary swear that this must be kept a secret and that the Cubs management could never find out about his hockey adventures with Schlitz and the gang.

Gary is a successful attorney now living in the Chicago suburbs. His law firm has four season tickets behind the Cubs dugout! A few years ago I went with him to a Cubs game, which led us to reminiscing.

"Those were the days! Hoisting my vending tray...must have weighed forty pounds! Bee-yah! Bee-yah!" said Gary with that far-away look in his eyes as he relived those days at Wrigley Field.

"Yes, but now you're an attorney with a real good law firm. Tell me, what's that like?" I asked.

"Sure," he shrugged, "what can I say? I like it alright, but I did have to take a pay cut from my vendor days at Wrigley Field."

Gary always had a witty sense of humor.

Understanding What It Means to be a Jew

The Chicago neighborhood where I grew up was about 40 percent Jewish. From what I understand, my father was from the tribe of Levi, the tribe of priests. My dad wanted me to understand what it meant to be a Jew, culturally and religiously. He signed me up for Hebrew School at Congregation Beth Shalom at age nine soon after we got settled in our new apartment. He wanted me to go to Hebrew School for five years and have a Bar Mitzvah at age thirteen. Having a Bar Mitzvah, or Bat Mitzvah for the girls, is an important ceremony for all observant Jews, whether they are orthodox, conservative, or even reformed.

From about ages nine to fourteen we would go to the synagogue on the high holidays and sometimes on the Sabbath. On Friday night after the service, we had what is called an *Oneg Shabbat* (after service fellowship). It is like a little meal after the service. During this time we had some pretty good food. The Rabbi would recite the prayers for the *challah* (bread) and for the wine and the good snacking. This consisted of Mogen David red wine, gefilta fish, red horseradish, *matzo* (unleavened bread), and special Jewish cookies. Good food is part of our culture. This was the Sabbath, a day of rest beginning on Friday at sundown until sundown on Saturday evening. I liked the Sabbath as long as I did not have to miss a baseball game.

I liked going to Hebrew school until my Bar Mitzvah. That last year from thirteen to fourteen seemed like an eternity because baseball was now more important. Your bar mitzvah is an event where all your family and friends come on a Saturday morning to the synagogue to hear you read a portion from the Torah and recite prayers. In Jewish culture, on this day you would begin to take on the responsibilities of a man. The Hebrew education was one aspect of this transition.

The services in our synagogue were somewhat boring to me as it was a bit ritualistic. This was more of a social event for me. I liked the food after Friday night and Saturday services, and I had a lot of friends in the synagogue. It was tolerable until I was fourteen years old. Then puberty hit; baseball and girls now become my first loves.

Sometimes during a break from our Hebrew School classes, my friends and I would go out back to the fenced in parking lot and play baseball. Sometimes even some of our gentile friends would join us for pickup games. We would play up against the wall of the synagogue. If you hit the ball over the fence it was a homerun. Our cantor, Emil Berkowitz, would sometimes join us in our games. Cantor Berkowitz had been a great baseball player as a teenager. He had been offered a minor league contract with the Los Angeles Dodgers, but decided not to take it because he did not want to break the Sabbath. He knew he would have to play ball on Saturdays and that was against his orthodox belief system. He opted to study to become a cantor, which also pleased his parents.

The cantor made this decision for his beliefs before a very well-known incident occurred which shook the entire baseball world. In the 1965 World Series, Sandy Koufax, the greatest pitcher in the game at that time, decided not to pitch in the opening game because it fell on Yom Kippur, the holiest day on the Jewish calendar. This could have adversely affected the outcome of the Series and his career, but Koufax believed his place was with his people that day. The Dodgers went on to win the Series in seven games, with Koufax pitching the final game on two day's rest. Koufax is to this day one of my heroes because of his stance to respect Yom Kippur (The Day of Atonement in the Torah) and the Jewish people.

As a young boy of ten years old, his stand for God and the Jewish people made me think about what it really meant to be a Jew.

My father and I shared a love for sports. We loved watching Cubs games on television and sometimes going to the games. After Koufax came another Jewish pitcher named Kenny Holtzman. He played for the Chicago Cubs. Holtzman won 174 games in the major leagues and threw two no-hitters. He pitched one time early in his career against Sandy Koufax and actually beat him 1-0. When I pitched for the University of Illinois from 1973-76, I learned from my coach, Lee Eilbracht, that Kenny pitched for him more than ten years earlier. I felt a bit of a Jewish connection through baseball.

Jewish Holidays

My brothers and I were very competitive, sports-loving kids, and a little on the wild side. We lived on the third floor of a three-flat. That was a big mistake, especially for our downstairs neighbors. We shared one bedroom in our three-bedroom apartment. We would slide our beds together and play football. I am sure they did not appreciate having three young maniacs bouncing around on beds on top of them. If our parents were gone, we would play hockey with spoons and bottle caps on the tile floor of the hallway. Sometimes, we froze a bagel and used it as a hockey puck with real hockey sticks in our long hallway.

We were full of fun and mischief, oblivious to how our behavior affected those around us. Our neighbors would knock on the door, upset and screaming for a little peace and quiet. We might knock it off for a while, but we would usually start right back up after a short break.

My brother Ricky was two and a half years younger than me, and my brother Bruce was almost five years younger. Rick and Bruce were a little closer to each other than I was to either of them. Rick took Bruce under his wing and they would try to antagonize me at times. I was a bit of a bully. I would chase them into my parents' bathroom and they would lock themselves in. I'd bang on the door while they tormented me from the other side. However, they both looked up to me, especially after I made my high school baseball team. They went on to be great athletes in high school and college. Rick was the captain of the basketball team and received a scholarship to play in Sheridan, Wyoming. Bruce went on to play football in college.

Bruce was born on Christmas day in 1959. Of course, Christmas did not mean very much to me in those days. It was nothing but a holiday that the gentiles celebrated, the birthday of their Messiah. In my home

49

we celebrated Hanukkah, The Festival of Lights, which lasts eight days, normally a week or two before Christmas. It marks the miraculous event of God making one day's worth of oil for the menorah last eight days in the holy temple in Jerusalem. In 165 B.C.E., Judah Maccabee defeated an overwhelming and numerically superior Greek army in the Battle of Emmaus. He thus liberated Jerusalem and purified the Temple, granting Jewish independence in the Holy Land for the first time in centuries.

For Jewish children, this is our time of receiving presents. Technically, we were supposed to receive one present for each day, but normally each child would receive one present and some socks and underwear. We lit the menorah candles each day. We played the dreidel, a top with a different Hebrew letter on each surface. Whoever spun it would have to put something in the pot or win something from it, depending on which letter was up when the dreidel fell.

I felt Christmas was an exclusive day for gentiles. It did nothing for me. When I saw children sitting on Santa's lap in a department store, I realized no Jewish child would do that. It felt weird to me when my mom took me to Marshall Field's department store in downtown Chicago during the holidays.

"Why don't you go up and tell Santa what you want to receive this year."

I grimaced at my mom. *What is she thinking? We're Jews, Mom. We don't do this. Besides for Hanukah, I get eight presents!*

"Mom, maybe I could invite Santa to our Hanukkah party. One bite of your potato pancakes, and he will come over to our side," I offered.

Sports and Girls

In eighth grade, my closest friends were Neal Siegel, Gary Steinberg, and Matthew Sullivan. Matthew was a gentile who played with me on my freshman and sophomore basketball teams at Loyola Park on Greenleaf and Sheridan Road. Another kid, Dennis Fredericks, was faster than any of us. When we did the fifty-yard dash, Dennis left the rest of us in the dust. He was blinding fast. Neal was exceptionally fast, but could never beat Dennis. I was fast myself, a step or two behind Neal.

That year the Blue-and-White football game was a big deal for all of us. Gary and I were to be the captain and co-captain. Matthew and Gary were the ends; and I was going to be our quarterback. Dennis Fredericks was the captain of the other team. Our main concern was that anytime Dennis could turn the corner, nobody could stop him before he hit the end zone. Dennis decided to play quarterback, which was somewhat of a relief, putting him behind the line of scrimmage rather than a few feet closer to the goal line.

There were also cheerleaders for this game. One of the cheerleaders for our team was a girl who was a year older than the rest of us. She must have been fourteen at the time, and I was not yet thirteen. Her name was Andrea Cohen. At least two of us, Gary and I, were crazy about Andrea. We both thought we were in love with her. We wanted to show off for the cheerleaders, but especially for Andrea, a very pretty girl who had big brown eyes, long brown hair, and olive tan skin.

The game was very close. With about one minute left, the game was tied. We came into the huddle with a couple of plays left in the game. I threw a pass to Matthew, our tall end, who grabbed it close to the goal line and was tagged before he could cross it. Within seconds of the game ending, we called time out. We had one play left and the whole school was out at the field watching.

Everyone was expecting me to throw the ball to Matthew again, so I said, "Gary, get ready. I'm going to come your way."

I threw the short pass to Gary in the end zone, and we went crazy as he caught the ball with no time left in the game. The spectators cheered and we were beside ourselves. We actually beat the White team and Dennis, one of our most talented and fierce competitors. He actually began to cry. He could not believe that his team had just lost. It was like losing the Super Bowl for him.

At the end of the game, we were trying to decide which one of us should ask Andrea for a date, Gary or I. After some talking, we decided that Andrea had been playing a game with us, flirting with both of us, playing us against each other. We decided that neither would ask her out, and that was the extent of our experience with girls in grade school.

In the winters, at Touhy Beach, called Leone Park, the Chicago Park District would come out, attach a fire hose to a hydrant, and create a skating pond. Neal, Gary, and I would get up early Saturday morning, bring our hockey sticks down to the pond, and play hockey. Some players had shin guards, others didn't. Someone usually had goalie equipment and a guy named Farrell Bulwa, who was a bit older than us, was usually that guy. Neal was a good player. He would later play hockey for the University of Illinois. This is how we would spend our winter Saturday mornings together.

A friend loves at all times,
and a brother is born for adversity.
(Proverbs 17:17 NIV)

**Jeff's Bar Mitzvah
picture at age 13**

**Jeff at age 14 with brothers,
Ricky (12) and Bruce (9)**

Thillens Baseball Stadium

Chapter 3:

Jeff, the Jock

Making the change from grade school to high school was an insecure time period for me. I wanted to be accepted, so I didn't let anyone know how insecure I really was. Since I was very prideful, I kept my feelings of inadequacy to myself. I was kind of torn up inside from my family life as well. I really wanted to do well in baseball, the one thing at which I excelled, the one thing that would not let me down. But some other aspects of the high school experience would prove to be less satisfying. I took classes, which were much harder than anything I had experienced.

During grade school, I always received good grades. I could get most of my work done while at school, and there really wasn't that much work to do, hardly anything to bring home. As a freshman, suddenly it wasn't nearly as easy to pull an A or a B. Now, we were supposed to bring our books home and complete our assignments. Many of the assignments I would get done by "borrowing" homework from my friends. I should just say steal the work of my friends. Rather than study and pay attention, I quickly copied assignments done diligently at home by studious friends when I got to school. When it was time for tests, I could sometimes catch the answers by looking over the shoulders of classmates who had actually studied. This was how I got through many of my classes, especially in my freshman year. However, my system was not exactly foolproof.

Algebra was very hard and math was my weak subject. My brain had a hard time coming to terms with how many Xs and Ys belonged on which side of the equal sign, and frankly I could not have cared less. What made it worse, the teacher had figured out a diabolical system, which prevented me from cheating in any way, shape or form. She appeared to me to be the twin sister of the Wicked Witch of the West. I would daydream about a tornado dropping out of the sky, carrying a nice little bungalow to drop on her head.

I didn't have the sense or the humility to ask Miss Straka to tutor me; so, on my first report card, I got a failing grade for algebra. My grades were terrible, complete with a D and two Cs. On the way home with my report card I thought of all the other places in the world I would rather be, including the bottom of Lake Michigan and the Cook County Jail.

When the moment came for my dad to set his eyes on the accomplishments of his learned oldest son, he threw the report card on the floor.

"I can't believe this," he said. "You could do a lot better than this. I am very disappointed."

Of course, I knew he was right, but that didn't keep me from failing algebra for the whole year. I was able to pull up some of the other grades, though. Altogether, my first year of higher learning made me realize that people actually had to study and do their *own* homework to make some kind of progress.

I was kicked off the baseball team because of my grades. One needed to maintain a C average to stay on the team. I was devastated until I was told I could make up my failing grade in algebra by attending summer school. I could not believe my good fortune. Instead of sleeping in, going to the beach or just hanging out with my friends, I could spend my mornings in a non-air-conditioned classroom enjoying those Xs, Ys, and equal signs that I had grown to love and cherish. I pulled a C, to replace my F, which gave me just a little worse than a C average for my first year of high school.

When I was a freshman in high school and unprepared for a test, I would sometimes fake illness. I would tell my mom I wasn't feeling good and needed to stay home from school. I was lying, but I figured that by staying home I could get some additional time to study.

One day, I was watching "Bozo's Circus," a popular children's show that played for years on Channel Nine. It came on just before the Cubs' home games, which were day games at the time. At the end of each show, they would play The Grand Prize Game, which pitted a fortunate young-ster with a ping-pong ball against a series of six buckets in front of him. The first bucket was easy, the second a little harder and so on, with the farthest bucket next to impossible. Even if the ball went right in, it would normally bounce out.

While I was watching, Mary Dorsey, our cleaning lady came into my room to clean. She said, "Mr. Siegel, what's wrong with you?" (It seemed like whenever I played hooky from school, it was Mary's cleaning day.)

I said to Mary, "I'm not feeling too good."

"Mr. Siegel, I'll lay hands on you and ask Jesus to heal you," Mary said.

I could tell that she believed what she said. I knew she had some sort of power in her life that I did not have and was afraid that I would really get healed and have to go back to school.

"No thanks, Mary," I said. "You don't have to pray for me."

"A day is coming, Mr. Siegel, when you are going to drop to your knees and ask Jesus into your heart. He will fill you with His Holy Spirit and make you brand new," she told me.

Mary was an illiterate black woman, who after becoming a Christian, went back to school to learn to read and write. She must have been about sixty years old when she went back to school. This impressed my family and me.

After having not been allowed to play on the baseball team during the spring of my freshman year because of poor grades, I vowed to pass every single class in my sophomore year. I was still getting a little help from my friends and classmates. One of my hard subjects was once again math. I had to work extra hard at it, but I was able to pull a C in Geometry. My homeroom teacher, Ms. Deverau was helpful in tutoring those who were struggling.

My junior and senior years I took Spanish. Spanish was also hard. Mr. Mukumbe, a Nigerian teacher, was pretty cool. Even though he would bring Motown records and show us how to do the penguin dance, I did not pay attention in class and once again got by with help from my friends. I got Cs in both years of Spanish.

I really enjoyed history taught by Mr. Glickman. When the subject of the Vietnam War came up, the discussions would sometimes become heated. There were two main groups at the school—the longhaired, dope-smoking heads, and the shorthaired, beer-drinking jocks. Some hybrids immerged like jocks who wore bell-bottomed pants, the standard issue for the flower children. The jocks tended to support the idea of Americans fighting in Vietnam, while the heads were dead against it.

While there were two groups or cliques, the jocks and the heads, there was a blurring of the lines. Even some of us jocks wore our hair a little longer, and those who favored the crew cuts that were popular a few years earlier were almost extinct. Four of us guys used to hang out together. We were all jocks, and all cocky as we could be: Gary Steinberg, Rich Rabinowitz, Steve Cohen, and me. (Years later Steven and his brother Irwin made the U.S. Judo Olympic Team.) We all bought white corduroy pants and smooth shirts, so we could perform dance routines together at parties to the sounds of the great soul groups like The Temptations. We even had our own strobe light, to heighten the effect of our performances.

One of our football coaches, Mr. Jacobson, who was from that age when men were men and didn't make their barbers stand around with nothing to do, used to ask me, "When are you going to get a haircut?"

Quite a few from his generation had an intense, seething hatred of anything remotely resembling long hair on men, which they equated with a lack of masculinity, rampant drug use, and disloyalty to the United States of America and everything for which it stands.

One day the coach said to me, jokingly, "If you lose today's game, you need to get a crew cut."

"That's not going to happen," I blurted out. "But if I win, how about if you get a crew cut."

His hair was closely cropped that season, because after I lost my first game, I won the next eight. Mr. Jacobson was glad to get his routine crew cut. I look back and realize that he probably would have made me come into the gym office, put a razor to my head, and given me a bald cut.

During my high school years, U.S. troops were being pulled out of Vietnam under President Nixon's Vietnamization policy, which meant turning the war over to our allies the South Vietnamese. This culminated in our enemies, the North Vietnamese, defeating our allies in April 1975, near the end of my junior year. Some of my classmates had older brothers who were drafted into the Army and fought in Vietnam, but by the time we got out of high school, the draft was over, and there was nothing left to protest.

It was some time in my junior year that I started thinking about going to college. Neal Siegel and some of my other friends were putting a little more time into their studies, and they began talking about going away to college.

Anti-Semitism

During the winter, I played basketball at the Loyola Park field house on a team with Neal and Gary. A group of gentile guys called themselves Patchers. They wore navy blue jackets and army boots. They were frequent shoppers at military surplus stores. One of them, whose last name was Murphy, played on the same team with us when we were freshmen. Now Murphy was on a team with the gentile guys. Just a couple of weeks earlier, a neighbor of mine had been beaten up by a group of these guys. Steve Wagner was a couple of years older than me and we sometimes played wall ball together in our back yard. They pummeled him. He came home with his eye the size of an egg. It really angered me that someone would do this just because a person was Jewish. Those thugs provided me with my first face-to-face encounter with anti-Semitism.

One day, as we entered the locker room to change for the game, Murphy called to his smirking buddies, "There are the Jews."

Then he turned to us, "Hey, Jew boys."

This was not an olive branch of friendship. It flashed across my mind what these guys had done to my neighbor and buddy, Steve. My hand curled into a fist. I smashed Murphy right in the lip. Blood was oozing from his lip. Murphy freaked out.

I continued into the locker room and began putting on my shorts. Fear began to creep in as I realized what I had just done. I wasn't so much afraid of Murphy, who already proved he was all talk, but I thought of his friends and feared that they might pummel me too after I left the park that night. I wondered how many people would be waiting for me once we finished our game.

Murphy came into the locker room. Putting his face close to mine, he growled, "I wanna fight you."

I could see fear in his eyes. I knew he was trying to act tough to save face with his thuggish friends.

I pushed him away and said, "Hey, Murphy, we used to play ball together on the same team. What's with the Jew-boy stuff?"

Taking a deep breath, I apologized for slugging him. I kept talking, trying to explain how offensive his taunts were to me. I could see he was angry. The guy who ran the park, found out what was going on and separated us.

Months later, I ran into Murphy again at an amusement park. Once again he challenged me to a fight, wanting to get revenge for his cut lip and prove his superiority. I wasn't so much afraid to fight Murphy, but some of his Nazi-loving friends had the reputation for being crazy. I thought one of them might pull a knife on me as Murphy asked me to leave the park with him. But amazingly some of the guys he was with that night had played little league with me. They told Murphy to leave me alone. I was very fortunate. God was watching over me.

That was the end of that situation, but not the end of my remembrance of how anti-Semitism affected my family. It was the stories of my father and grandfather, who also experienced a measure of anti-Semitism, which fueled my reaction to Murphy's comments. There is a rallying call of Jews everywhere, especially Israelis, who have lived in the shadow of Auschwitz and other death camps.

Inside every Jewish man and woman who understands what we have suffered as a people is the resounding cry, "Never Again."

I remember when I was a little boy, I noticed that my grandfather was getting mail from relatives in Romania.

I asked my Grandpa Jack, "Would you like to go back and visit with your relatives?"

"No! That is the last place on earth I would ever return to," he told me in a loud voice with his old country accent, typical of so many older Jewish people in the neighborhood.

I asked, "Why?"

Then my grandpa shared with me what it was like for him growing up in Romania.

"It is so much different from America. In Romania we had *pogroms*. A *pogrom* is where gentiles would gather Jewish people together like animals, beat them up and persecute them. Sometimes they would even kill Jewish people," he explained. My grandfather told me a story of a time when he and his sister were forced to hide in their wine cellar while a *progrom* was taking place outside their home.

Like so many American Jews of his generation, he came to America to escape persecution a few decades before Hitler began his extermination of Jews throughout most of Europe. Millions wanted to escape the prejudice and ill treatment that had developed. They were willing to experience the dangerous and miserable journey by boat across the Atlantic Ocean to arrive in what they believed to be the new Promised Land in the United States of America.

My Senior Year

My senior year, I was attracted to a girl named Cheryl. She was a cute blonde Jewish girl and I was very fond of her. I went out on a few dates with her and my friends; we liked going to see the Temptations sing at the Mill Run Theater in the suburbs. We also went indoor roller-skating with friends. I was a senior and Cheryl was a sophomore and knew that I was preparing for college. I think that she figured that I was going away, and it was not worth investing in a long distance relationship.

I had a friend, Howie Krisberg, who could do imitations of actors like James Cagney, Jimmy Durante, and Ed Sullivan and was pretty good. He was sprouting sideburns and chest hair when he was fourteen. He looked like an ape. Howie was totally cool with his sideburns and ape-like chest and back. How I longed to have sideburns like him. My senior year I sprouted a single hair on my chin. That was a big deal. However, I just had this one lonely hair on my chin. By the end of my senior year, that one hair found some company. During the summer, sideburns began to take root. Life was good.

The good Lord must have been watching over me in those years. My senior year, I was out with a guy named, Gary Kleiner, who was a pretty good basketball player but not on the team. He was a good example of someone who was a jock and a head. We were out in his car, going to meet some girls. He pulled out a marijuana joint and handed it to me. I had never smoked marijuana before and it really hit me hard. I felt like I had no control over myself, and I didn't like the feeling at all. I was very afraid. I actually started hallucinating. I looked at a clock and it looked like things were growing out of the clock and out of the ceiling when we arrived at Gary's house. The room we were in at Gary's home had a black light and psychedelic posters. It was a very frightening experience. Gary somehow got me home that night. I don't know how Gary was able to drive his car without getting us killed.

Not far from where I grew up was a suburb called Evanston. We liked going to a well-manicured toboggan hill that we called "Mount Trashmore" because it was built on top of a massive garbage dump. I would go up there with Steve Freskos, our team's shortstop, and a couple of girlfriends and drink Seagram's™ 7 and 7-Up˚. We would get drunk and hang out on top of Mount Trashmore. Those were the kind of things we would do late in high school. I am grateful that we did not get killed in a car accident going home.

During that year, a guy we knew from high school, Jordy Schulgasser, who played on the basketball team with Gary Steinberg, invited a few of us to his fraternity house at the University of Illinois, Tau Epsilon Phi. TEPS, as it was commonly known, was a mostly Jewish frat house, a huge house on fraternity row, in a neighborhood just west of the main campus that is home to dozens of frat and sorority houses. The Greek system was a big part of the University of Illinois. Gary and I had a great weekend. We decided to go to the University of Illinois and to join the fraternity.

The eyes of the Lord are everywhere,
keeping watch on the wicked and the good.
(Proverbs 15:3 NIV)

**Growing up in Chicago on Farwell Avenue;
our apartment is on the 3rd floor, left-hand side**

**Farwell Beach, Lake Michigan-
2 blocks from our apartment, Chicago skyline**

Chapter 4:

On Top of the World

When I was three years old, my dad began to teach me how to play baseball. He was a very good baseball and softball player. I remember watching him on Sundays in Morton Grove, Illinois. Dad would play softball with a ball that was sixteen inches around. It was called a clincher and at the beginning of the game a new ball was very hard. This game was played with bare hands, no gloves. A ball hit hard to the third baseman could scorch your hands. My father played mostly center field. He was extremely fast, had a great arm, and actually had a little power for a guy 5 foot 9 inches. I became friends with the children of some of the other players. We used to play with bats and balls on the sidelines during the games.

I began little league at Pottawattamie Park at eleven years old. I was a pitcher, the number one or two on my team. I also played the outfield because I was a fast runner. Sometimes I played shortstop or second base as well. I was a line-drive hitter with a little pop in my bat. I usually batted number two as I rarely struck out.

One of my first teams was the Little League Cubs. My coach let me pitch, and I was one of the only kids with a curve ball. I was playing catch with my friends one day at Morton Grove when I grabbed the ball by the seams and began to spin the ball. It began to curve to the side. I could make it go down as well.

Apart from little league, there was an asphalt baseball diamond on our schoolyard at Eugene Field School. We would play baseball with rubber balls, the same size and color as major league balls. We would get them for a quarter at the local drugstore. Sometimes we would play all day along, taking a bag lunch and going to the schoolyard at 9:00 a.m.

Imagine eighteen to twenty kids playing a game of baseball on the asphalt. At times, we would start the game with people missing from fielding positions and an hour later we would have them filled. We had Gary Shulman, who became a lawyer and lives in the Chicago suburbs; Neal Siegel, who has a successful Christian marketing firm; David Mulligan, who played college basketball; Mike Aiello; a guy named Tom (Weasel) Zielsky; the famous Farrell Bulwa, the one with the goalie's equipment; Rick Plotkin; Sherwin Crown; Gary Steinberg; Gary Cohen; Matthew Sullivan; Dennis Fredricks, who had blinding speed; Billy Carmel; Ricky Monky, who was Dennis Fredricks' cousin and also very fast; and Jeff Sutton, to name a few.

We would go to the local drug store called Mitch's, a few blocks away on Lunt Avenue, for a fountain coke and bring our bag lunch or get a hot dog. Then after lunch, we would go back and play again. When school was out, we could just play days on end because we loved baseball so much.

When I was twelve years old, I was blessed with good speed, a strong accurate arm, and good hand-eye coordination, which are essential for hitting a baseball. That year I had a good season. My only problem was that I was one of the smaller kids. I would always have to work harder and show better skills to the coaches than someone bigger. My dad encouraged me to work hard practicing the fundamentals that the coaches would show us in practice. I felt that all things being equal someone bigger would get the nod from the coach.

My dad would grab a baseball glove and I would practice my pitching. He coached me a lot in pitching. I practiced my fastball and curve ball throwing them into my father's glove. We practiced in our back alley behind our garage about once or twice a week. Of course, I would also practice with my friends and coaches as well.

After a game, as we were approaching midseason, my coach told me that I was selected for the All Star Team and that the All Star Game would be played at Thillens Stadium on Devon and Kedzie Avenue. I had only seen Thillens from the outside while switching buses right in front of the stadium when traveling from my home to see my grandparents. Whenever I had to stop at Thillens, I would walk up to this stadium and peek in the cracks dreaming of the day I would play in this stadium. At Thillens, they had a front and back stadium. The one in front was beautiful with grass outfield and infield and they even had lights for night games.

A currency exchange company created Thillens and modeled the stadium after a big league park, with dugouts, grandstands, a well-groomed field, and concession stands. They even called your name on loudspeakers when they announced the lineup and when you came up to bat. This was nothing like Pottawattamie Park, which had backstops, bumpy infields and park benches, with not enough space on them for the entire team.

We were playing the Pottawattamie League Champions the Tigers from the year before. They had a nifty shortstop named Steve (The Greek) Freskos. He was a fantastic shortstop, a tiny bit shorter than me and very quick. Anything near him, he was going to field it. We called him the "Vacuum Cleaner." He ended up playing on our high school team and later was the captain of the baseball team at the University of Illinois Circle Campus.

The game was seven innings, and all of our parents and families were there. It was like the World Series. I loved baseball so much. It was even more of a form of worship for me than going to the synagogue.

I was put into the game in the bottom of the fifth inning as a pinch hitter, and we were losing 4-3, but we had runners on second and third with one out. My heart was thumping as I stood in the on deck circle. I picked up two bats and began to loosen up as my name was announced, "Next batter for the Pottawattamie All Stars, Jeff Siegel."

I had the opportunity to get the go-ahead hit. I knew the Tigers' pitcher, a kid named Tim with blond hair and glasses, who had a hard, straight fastball. I had hit against him many times in my years in little league. He always pitched fast and straight and down the middle. I decided that I was going to go after his first pitch. I stepped into the batter's box and his pitch came just as I had expected, a straight fastball heading toward the middle of the plate about waist high. I swung hard and the bat connected with the ball and the next thing I knew the ball was heading over the head of the shortstop into left center field. One runner home from third and the second was safe sliding into home. The crowd cheered; I was on first with a line drive single.

This pitcher retired the rest of our team and I went to play right field. I had one ball hit to me and I was taken out the next inning. We went on to win the game 5-4. What a thrill for me. I was on cloud nine.

My parents treated me to my after game meal at a local hot dog place called Fluky's. Their famous Chicago-style dogs oozed mustard and ketchup from a steamed poppy seed bun. The wiener nestled among the relish, kosher dill, and a pepper. While popping the ever-famous piece of gum shaped like a hot dog into my mouth, I realized that baseball would be a major part of my life.

During my time on the eleven to twelve-year olds' team, the Cubs had two good pitchers, Dewey Robinson and me. Dewey was our number one pitcher and I was number two. Dewey was a good kid from an athletic family and always dreamed of pitching in the major leagues. We were on the Cubs for one year together, and then the Yankees picked up Dewey. I especially got excited about playing the Yankees and Dewey. When we played against each other, my team usually won. Dewey and I made our high school team. I was one year ahead, but we were the same age. Dewey grew faster than me and started from his freshman year. I did not start playing until my junior year.

Senior Year at Sullivan High

My senior year at Sullivan High, I made the starting team in baseball. During the summer league at Winnemac Park, I had a good season hitting about .333. I knew we were going to have a good senior season with Dewey Robinson, who was emerging as an unhittable pitcher, as the ace of our staff. A high school team, which plays two games a week or so, can rely on two good starting pitchers if they stay healthy. With a future major leaguer at the top of the list, there was a lot of competition for the number two spot.

We had a Japanese American guy named, Kevin Maruyama, who also played little league at Pottawattamie Park. We also had a left-hander named, Aren Porec, who threw pretty hard. He was a good hitter as well. So, I had my work cut out for me if I was going to be the other starter. Aren Porec became our number two, but didn't get off to a great start. In a game against Von Steuben High School, he got bombed. I came in from the bullpen and had a good outing. I struck out several batters, including some guys I had been friends with when I lived in Albany Park as a boy. I also hit a double into right field in that game.

I was so cocky that I began smiling at the other team. The Von Steuben players were calling me "Smiley." It provoked them to see me smirking on the mound, gloating. They began hitting me pretty hard, and I was pulled for Dewey. Von Stuben won the game by one run. At our team meeting the next day, Coach Jonesy scolded me for my attitude.

I was the losing pitcher that game, but I won eight games in a row after that. I took Coach Jonesy's advice. I really respected Coach Jonesy and I learned a valuable lesson.

"When you are on the mound," he said, "you don't show any emotion. You don't smile at the other team. You don't do anything to wake them up. You go out there and work hard and stay stone-faced."

I had an 8-1 win-loss record going into the playoffs; Dewey had 13 wins and 2 losses. We made it to the semi-finals of the city public high school championship. We played another north side school called, Taft. The winner would advance to the championship game in Comiskey Park, home of the Chicago White Sox. Taft used Kelly Ozurk, who later pitched at Illinois State University. We went with Dewey, who like all of us, desperately wanted to get passed Taft to play in a major league ballpark.

We were not a great hitting team, but our pitching was our strong point, backed by a very tight defense. I was playing second base that day because my coach did not want me to strain my arm if he needed me in relief. I was a good hitter; the coach wanted my bat in the lineup. I got on base by a walk and stole second. I was hoping someone would drive me in, but I died on second base.

Taft pitcher, Ozurk, ruined our hopes of playing on the nation's oldest big league diamond by shutting out our team, holding us to one hit in seven innings. Dewey did not let us down, pitching a two-hitter. Taft scored once, defeating us by the slimmest margin. It was a heartbreaker. The following year, Sullivan made it to the city series at Comiskey Park. Dewey pitched very well in that game, and the number two starter for Sullivan, Aren Porec, hit two triples, but they lost that game.

The following year, Dewey went to Southern Illinois on a baseball scholarship. He played for Itch Jones, who later became head coach at the University of Illinois, where he also coached future major leaguers, Darrin Fletcher and Scott Spiezio. Dewey later pitched SIU into the College World Series. After college, the Chicago White Sox drafted Dewey. He pitched games against the New York Yankees and actually pitched against guys like Reggie Jackson from 1979 to 1981. He was possibly the only ball player from Rogers Park—which produced thousands of serious young athletes—to join the exclusive club of big league players.

The summer after graduating from high school, I played on an American Legion team with Dewey and other high school and college players. My record that summer was 8 and 0. Dewey and a Lane Tech pitcher were the one-two starters on the team. We played a lot of games. I was used as a starter and reliever. I worked very, very hard and had a great year. It was a dream of mine to go to school at the University of Illinois, especially so I could be with some of my buddies, like Gary Steinberg and Neal. I had improved my grades by my senior year, so now I was a C-plus student. I knew my grade-point average was not going to get me into any of the more selective colleges, like the business school, so I applied for the physical education program and got in.

My dad had been against me going away to school at first, because of financial issues.

"Please don't make me go to the Chicago Circle Campus," I said, referring to the university's Chicago commuter campus. "I think I will do a lot better if I go away for school."

He made a deal with me.

"I will get you a job at Marshall Field's," he said. "If you can sell shoes all summer and do well, I will pay the difference in your education."

Heading for College

A lot of the guys I hung out with in the neighborhood who were at the University of Illinois were living at Tau Epsilon Phi Fraternity house, which was mostly Jewish. Even though these guys knew how to have a good time, many of the forty fraternity brothers were studying to become doctors, lawyers or business executives. So, they kept their grade-point averages up, with most of them staying in the 3.5 to 4.0 range, with 4 point being a perfect "A" average. The guys helped each other with a system of saving and filing their papers, so the older students and past students could help out the younger ones. That also appealed to me, knowing that I was such a weak student in high school.

Although it was a Jewish fraternity house, exceptions were made. My roommate was Carl Kemner, a blue-eyed, blonde-haired German American, who somehow managed to fit in. He was a very good student, a member of the fencing team, and very well liked.

Even though I was at the physical education college, not known as the most challenging curriculum, I was deathly afraid that I might flunk out. So, during my freshman year, I started paying attention in class, actually studying, and working on the assignments. I had confidence in my ability as an athlete, especially as a baseball player, but I didn't go out for the team as a freshman because I wanted to focus on getting decent grades.

I'm not saying that I never cheated on a test in college, but I was taking it a lot more seriously than I ever had in high school.

Amazingly, my thinking on school began to change, I actually decided I wanted to get something out of my education.

Every day after dinner, I went to the library to study. Starting out in my college career, I had a bad case of déjà vu when I cracked open my old nemesis—the algebra textbook. But I had a very good teacher, and I shared with him that I was frightened to death of not doing well. He offered to tutor me. Between his help and my roommate, Carl, helping me, I was able to pull a B. I really worked hard and actually earned this grade. My first semester, I actually made the Dean's List, which meant I had about a 3.2 average on a 4 point scale.

Robert Cline

Another gentile member of the fraternity, a young man from New Jersey, would later play a significant role in my life and the lives of many young people. He was about 6-foot-3, 240 pounds of solid rock muscle, an accomplished athlete and a friendly, charismatic guy. Everyone voted unanimously to accept him into the fraternity house. Most of the brothers were honored that such a big man on campus would want to live with us. He was at the university on a football scholarship, but also played on the baseball team. His name was Robert Cline. His ethnic background was French, German, and Syrian. Robert and I had a lot in common, especially our love for sports.

Robert was a really likeable guy, who was a bit homesick when I first met him. He told me that he was drafted out of high school to play for the New York Mets, but decided to go to college instead because of his love of football. He was deciding between Penn State and the University of Illinois, but chose Illinois because a former Dartmouth Ivy League Coach named Bob Blackman recruited him to come to Champaign to play football. While Robert came to the U of I on a football scholarship, Lee Eilbracht, the baseball coach, heard that he had been drafted by the Mets out of high school and talked him into coming out for the baseball team.

My freshman year, I pulled good grades and returned home for the summer to spend the second summer selling ladies shoes at Marshall Field's, the city's historical downtown store. Robert had invited me to visit his home in Clifton, New Jersey. I went to see Robert the last week of the summer vacation.

One evening at the Cline house, I met Robert's brother, David. I was eating a TV dinner and he stuck his finger in my mashed potatoes and ate some. Then he introduced himself. That was the beginning of a friendship that endured for many years, but inevitably crashed when a tragedy hit our lives.

I played American Legion ball the summer of my freshman year. One of my former rival teams was called Mather High School. Their center fielder Ronnie Lapins was one year older than me. He made the University of Illinois team his freshman year. During Legion ball, Ronnie encouraged me to come out for the university team.

"Jeff," he said, "You can play at this level. I recommend that you come out as a pitcher."

In high school when I wasn't pitching, I played the outfield and second and third base. In college I had to decide whether I was going to be a pitcher or an everyday player. By my sophomore year, I had grown to a whopping 5-foot-8-inches and weighed 155 pounds. I decided I would have the best chance of making the team as a pitcher.

At my frat house, we did a lot of crazy and wrong things. There was a lot of marijuana, alcohol, and other drugs used by some of the brothers. We invited bands to our house and had big parties, with kegs of beer always on hand, as well as whiskey and plenty of joints. Sometimes high school girls would come to our wild parties. I took part in most everything that was going on, but avoided marijuana because of my bad experience in high school.

During my second year, Robert and I double-dated one evening. My date was gorgeous. At the beginning of our date, she offered me some brownies. She explained to me that one of the main ingredients was marijuana.

Although my first experience with marijuana was a nightmare, I reasoned, "How potent could brownies be?"

Of course, I wanted to appear cool and fearless to my drop dead gorgeous date. It didn't take long before I realized this was another terrible mistake. I became very quiet, and had the feeling of being emotionally paralyzed. What started out as a promising date, ended up as one of the worse nights of my life. I then added eating marijuana to the list of things I would never do again.

My Sophomore Year

My sophomore year in college, I was selected to represent the University of Illinois baseball team and go on the spring trip to Edinburg, Texas. I was a fine-tuned athlete, but I also liked the parties. I didn't really like drinking beer, but I enjoyed the atmosphere of getting a little buzz off of beer. At Pan-American University in Edinburg, a group of us ballplayers hatched a plan. We stole the coach's car and drove across the border into Mexico, to a small city called Reynosa. We took some sorority girls across the border with us. We went to a bar and went dancing. We somehow snuck the coach's car back into his space without him discovering what we had done. Had the coach found out what we had done, we would have been kicked off the team and perhaps out of school.

In my first game on the road for the University of Illinois, I got knocked around, and there were some fielding mishaps behind me. It was not a good start. The next time I came in, I did better. When we got back to Illinois, I was slated as a reliever. As I did well in this role, I found myself starting in games outside our conference. My record blossomed to 3-0 going into the final game in the Big Ten.

In our final game of the year, Iowa was playing for the Big Ten Conference Championship. At the end of the fifth inning in our second game of a double header, I was brought in the game as relief. I got the side out. We tied the game the bottom of the seventh and last inning. Ron Lapins got on base and Robert drove him in with a double. Everyone went crazy. We won 5 to 4 that day.

I was 4 and 0, with an 0.35 ERA, which meant I let up just one earned run in twenty-six innings. The coach was very happy with my performance for the year.

Coach Eilbracht took me aside after the game and said, "Next year you'll be in the starting rotation. I will see that you get a partial scholarship for your good season."

On Top of the World

The scholarship eased some of the financial burden for my junior year. I felt that the scholarship showed my dad that going to the U of I was a good decision.

Now I was on top of the world. I was very proud of myself, and my family was very proud of me.

I had about a B average my sophomore year. Not that I stopped cheating altogether. I copied from someone else on an occasional test. Plagiarizing a paper, saying it was my own, was rather a common occurrence in our frat house. Of course, this was morally and ethically wrong. I thought at the time I was a good guy, and justified my actions saying to myself that everyone does this to some degree.

I had it made. I was going out with a lot of girls. I had lots of friends, including many of my fraternity brothers. I was at my dream school. I was on scholarship for baseball. I received a letterman's sweater at the end of my sophomore year. I wore that on campus and really thought I was a big shot.

I used to frequent a lot of bars on campus. One of my favorites was White Horse Inn, which had live music, including some great soul groups. I would go there with Robert Cline and some of my other friends. We would dance the night away. I loved baseball a lot, but it was extremely competitive. If you didn't work on your game and your body all the time, you were not going to be able to compete with some of the best players in college baseball.

Disappointment

Our University of Illinois pitching coach, Pete Sharton, played with the Boston Red Sox as a pitcher. He really was a good pitching coach.

Because of my good sophomore season, Pete wanted me to pitch in the Cape Cod League during the summer. He felt that I had the credentials to pitch in this illustrious league. He sent my credentials to the Yarmouth Red Sox. They wrote back that they needed one relief pitcher and they thought that I could fill the bill. I was so excited at this possibility. You worked during the day and played games at night. Dewey Robinson was also going to play in this league and already had been accepted by a team as a starter.

Right before the summer season started, the Yarmouth Red Sox filled this spot with someone else. It really broke my heart. This league attracts many major league scouts and the competition is great. Some of the best college players in the country go to the Cape Cod League with the hope of being scouted and drafted to a major league team. This was an incredible disappointment for me. I was at the top of my game and wanted to play against some of the best college players, but it was not to be.

When I returned home for the summer, I began to witness the unraveling of my parents' marriage. Their arguments were becoming nastier and more frequent. The apartment on Farwell Avenue was the last place I desired to return to. That summer I played on a semi-pro team called the Pottawattamie Indians. It was a college-level summer team. (By now, the home field was much improved from the rock-strewn diamonds we used in little league.)

One hot, muggy night we were playing on our home field. The small park sits one mile west of Lake Michigan adjacent to some raised commuter railroad tracks. That night a cold breeze rolled in off the lake, suddenly dropping the temperature 15-20 degrees. This can be common when you live close to Lake Michigan. I was not wearing long sleeves beneath my jersey that night because it was so hot when the game began. I could feel the wind chilling my elbow.

I had thrown a lot of hard sliders and curve balls, along with my fastball. Suddenly, I could feel the tendons tensing up. My elbow froze up and I was in a lot of pain. I hoped that with a hot shower and an ice pack I would be okay in time for my next start. But about four days later when I was warming up, I could still feel the pain coursing through my elbow. Even when I threw an easy fastball, I could feel the pain. By the end of the summer season, my arm had healed to a degree. I could throw fastballs, but when I went to throw a breaking pitch, there was pain. I pitched some of the last games of the season in pain.

I returned to selling shoes at Marshall Field's and was making good money, as I was a commissioned salesman. I met a girl at work named Carol. She was a very pretty blonde. Carol attended St. Mary's of Notre Dame in South Bend, Indiana. We began to date. She was a soft-spoken Catholic girl and pleasant to be with. We had a lot of fun dating and spending time with friends, going dancing and to movies. Carol lived in the suburbs of Chicago about thirty minutes from my house. When I wanted to go out on a date with Carol, my dad made it difficult. He always had an excuse why I could not use his car, only letting me use it on a limited basis. My dad was a very prejudiced man. He made it very clear that he never wanted me to marry a non-Jewish woman.

One of our department management personnel, Chuck, graduated from Notre Dame. He had a brother named, Mike. Mike played on the Notre Dame football team. Chuck introduced me to him and we became friends. Mike told me that anytime I wanted to come to Notre Dame and see Carol, I could stay in his room for the weekend and see the basketball and football games. When the summer ended, Carol and I agreed that we would come to see each other at Notre Dame and the University of Illinois.

Regaining My Pop

When I returned to college for my junior year, I went to the physical therapy clinic inside of Freer Gym. The man who ran it set up conditioning programs for the baseball players. The physical therapist was Aaron Mattis, and he diagnosed my arm as having a hyperextended elbow.

His solution, "You are going to have to do special exercises to heal your elbow."

It turned out to be a blessing in disguise. He taught me how to do exercises in many parts of my body in addition to shoulder routines, special exercises for my elbow and weight lifting to build endurance. My elbow made a clicking noise. He said there was some scar tissue built up. We would have to break it down and pull that elbow back until it was no longer hyper extended. He wanted to break down the adhesions in my elbow to bring full healing. After several months, my arm and body were feeling strong. There is an expression in pitching regarding coming back after an injury; I needed to "regain my pop."

I threw about eighty mph. I was not an exceptionally fast pitcher, but threw hard for a guy my size. I was still about five feet, eight inches tall and weighed 155 pounds. My fastball would tail in on right-handed batters. It had a natural tail because my delivery was between three-quarters and side-arm. My forte was my breaking ball, a slider that broke over the outside corner and a curve ball that really dropped. Occasionally, I would throw a knuckleball, a ball thrown slowly without any natural spin to it, which flutters here and there, letting the air current's action on the seams take it in various directions, which leave batters in a state of perplexity.

During my rehab, I decided to go to Notre Dame and see Carol. There was a bus that went to South Bend Indiana and I stayed with my friend, Mike. He got me tickets to the Notre Dame basketball and football games.

Carol and I went to the games and had a good time. Leaving to go back to the University of Illinois was hard and so was a long distance relationship.

During our winter inside practice sessions, I was pitching well. I felt that I had been rehabbed and was one of the four starting pitchers on our spring trip to New Mexico. We left for the University of New Mexico at the beginning of the month of March. The stadium was close to the mountains of Santa Fe. When it came my turn to pitch, it was very cold. I was not a good cold weather pitcher. The altitude was high and the air was thin. This was an adjustment for our whole team. I had learned to throw on the batters' fists in high school. But in college, they used aluminum bats instead of wooden ones; they were lighter than wooden bats. They also had a larger sweet spot. The lighter bats eliminated the pitcher's advantage because hitters could whip them around much quicker. I was wild in my first start in the tournament, and I was removed from that game.

We were playing in a minor league stadium (which was also the home of the University of New Mexico Lobos). It must have been about fifty degrees that day. I was wild and I walked the bases loaded. Then the other team got a hit off me. They began to score some runs. I had never pitched that badly. Coach Eilbrach came out to the mound and put his hand out for the baseball.

He said, "Jeff, if you can't get the ball over the plate, you cannot pitch for this institution."

I was deeply shaken. I tried to hide the feeling of panic I felt. The coach handed the ball back to me. After that I was able to pitch some strikes, but we still lost the game. The statement "not pitching for this institution" was still ringing in my ears, and would continue to haunt me in the weeks and months to come.

My sophomore season, I had enjoyed a season of tremendous success. I had been written up in the newspapers. I had proudly worn my baseball

U of I team T-shirt when I went out to the bars and fraternity parties with my buddies. Then, in a moment, all my success seemed on the verge of sprouting wings and flying off somewhere, never to return in my lifetime. It really hit me that everything you had in life, your ability, your popularity, could all be taken away from you in a moment. Life is so fleeting. That really rocked me.

Remember how fleeting is my life.
(Psalm 89:47 NIV)

**University of Illinois Baseball Picture of
Jeff Siegel in 1976 (21 years old)**

Jeff visits Tau Epsilon Phi fraternity house
where he stayed during his years at the
University of Illinois.

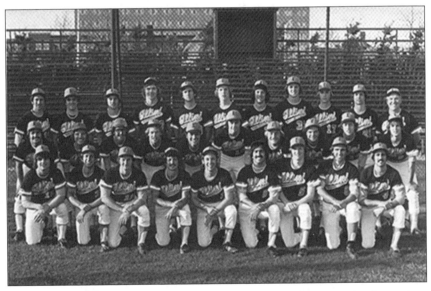

University of Illinois Baseball Team Picture (1977. Jeff is in the front row,
4th from the right; Jr. Varsity Head Coach and Assistant Varsity Coach

Chapter 5:

God and Who?

During our tournament at the University of New Mexico, I had the opportunity to relief pitch the last inning of a game we were winning by a couple of runs. I held off the other team and we won. I was pretty happy with the result.

My roommate on the trip, Robert Cline, came to me after the game and said, "Billy Graham is speaking tonight at a crusade. I would really like to go hear him speak. Would you go with me?"

"Thanks for inviting me," I responded, "but I'll take a rain check. Why don't you tell me what he says?"

Instead, I went out with some other friends on the team. We went out disco dancing the night away. We met some girls from sororities in the area, and we went out to the local bars. That was my way of having fun in those days. And besides, Jewish kids from Chicago didn't go to gentile religious gatherings.

Later that night, back in the room, Robert came in and said, "I got saved tonight."

Unimpressed I asked, "What did you get saved from?"

Robert said, "I became a Christian tonight."

This caught me by surprise because Robert went to church on Sundays when we were on campus. I didn't understand how a Christian could become a Christian.

He had an answer.

"Mr. Graham made me realize that just going to church didn't make me a Christian. Just because a mouse is in a cookie jar doesn't make it a cookie. He made me realize that I needed to have a personal relationship with God through Jesus Christ. I asked Jesus to forgive me for my sins. I asked him into my heart," Robert explained. "I'm a born-again Christian now."

He sat down on his bed and leaned toward me, "Jeff, you need to be born again, too."

He explained that you need a spiritual rebirth by confessing Jesus as your Lord and Savior and inviting him into your heart. But I was more into going out and having fun. Besides that, I was Jewish. Nothing he was talking about could possibly have anything to do with me.

After my good relief outing at the University of New Mexico, I began to start games but I did not do well. I lost one game after another. I was really in a valley and could not find a way to get my pitching on the right track again. I felt my previous injury had something to do with why my pitching was suddenly worse than ever. But whether it did or not, I had no clue how to fix the problem. I was having a terrible year. I lost my starting job and now I was back to relief. I was disappointed that I had been demoted to relief, but the coach is going to go with the person who is most effective in a short season. I had a one and two record for the season. My ERA soared to 7.08 in twenty-two innings pitched and my control was off. I walked twenty batters in twenty-two innings and hit five batters. The year before I walked five batters in twenty-six innings and allowed only seventeen hits.

Baseball was everything to me. It was truly my god, and playing, especially playing well, was the closest thing to worship that I knew at that time.

> *But there was something stirring in me, telling me that there must be more to life than just being a baseball player.*

I returned home for the summer after my junior year. My grades were pretty good, about 3.0 out of 4.0. I continued to work at Marshall Field's in downtown Chicago and to date Carol. This was somewhat of a pivotal summer. The previous two summers I had played on Legion and Semi Pro Teams. But the summer before going into my senior year, I took some time to rest my body from all the years of pitching and playing the game. This actually proved to be a very positive move going into my senior season.

In the fall of my senior year, I met a beautiful Jewish girl named, Wendy, from Skokie, a predominantly Jewish suburb just northwest of Rogers Park. We began to date at that time. I broke off the long-distance relationship with Carol. Because of religious conflict, me being Jewish and she being Catholic, I felt that it would be better to go out with a Jewish girl who I was even fonder of. I was a senior and Wendy was a sophomore. I liked her so much that I gave her my fraternity pin. In the fraternity system, it is almost like a pre-engagement type of thing. After going out with her for almost a year, I asked her what my chances were if I asked her to marry me.

"If you ask me to marry you, I will say *yes*," she replied.

On one hand, that was a good thing. But I was a little frightened, as I felt empty inside, realizing I was not ready for marriage. I did not have a sense of purpose in life. I needed some answers.

Wendy's family had a clothing business. They were members of a country club. I admired her family. They seemed to have a measure of wealth. I also had some wealthy relatives, but my parents were not in that financial class. We were an average, middle class family.

Turning Point

I was beginning to see the life ahead for me, and it did not really look that great. Within the Jewish community, there was a lot of pressure to be an accomplished person who made a lot of money: a successful businessman, a doctor, a lawyer, or some kind of professional person. It was understood within my family and community that this was going to be your lifestyle. But down deep, I did not see the purpose in this way of life. I thought, *if I become a businessman and make a lot of money, I will just be doing something that somebody else already did. What am I supposed to do that would be unique for me? I had no real sense of direction.*

Questions swirled in my brain.
Does God have a plan for my life?
Why was I born anyway?
Why was I born Jewish?
Is this a good thing?
Is this a bad thing?
If we are His chosen people, what were we chosen for?
How can I get right with God? How?
What are God's feelings about me?
It was at this time that the biblical truths that my friends were planting in my heart began to grow. What does Jesus have to do with all of this?
Is He the Jewish Messiah?
Was He just a man, a rabbi, a prophet?
Who is this man?

It was at this time that the biblical truths my friends were planting in my heart began to grow. I remembered the stories I learned in Hebrew School about Moses and Abraham. Moses was a most humble man, and Moses had a burning bush experience. At that point, God revealed his life's purpose to him. God told him to return to the children of Israel and lead them out of Egypt.

With my last name being Siegel (originally Segal), I've been told I'm from the same tribe as Moses, the tribe of Levi. I began to question if I should be a physical education teacher, or if God had a different plan for my life. I wondered if I should marry Wendy. I realized that if I did, I would then have the same pressures that every Jewish man has: to earn a lot of money in order to have two or three nice new cars and a big house. However, I had no idea why I was even born. It was like having a mid-life crisis at age twenty-one. I did not need to see the flames in the bush before I realized that I was not cut out for the traditional path.

Wendy and I got along beautifully. She was willing to marry me and that was something I once wanted more than anything in the world. If I had to point to one turning point in our relationship, I would say it was the day I was at her home, speaking to her mother. She had been out golfing that day at her country club.

"How was your golf game?" I asked her.

"I played terribly," she said.

She acted as if having a bad round of golf was something of cataclysmic importance.

I sensed that there was something much deeper going on than just a bad day on the links. I realized she was a very unhappy person. I wondered why someone who seemed to have everything would be so unhappy. She had a kind, generous husband, two nice cars, and a comfortable home. I began to observe that these things in themselves did not bring joy.

I ended up breaking up with Wendy, who had seemed to be the love of my life just a few months earlier. I needed to be apart from her to make some big decisions about my future. It was one of the toughest times of my life.

I knew that I was not happy myself. When I realized that fullness of joy did not lie at the end of the path of wealth and success, I was left with a terrible empty feeling. I knew that having things and a great job is not wrong. But I saw that some people who have everything really have nothing.

I began to realize that being successful and the things that success could afford do not necessarily bring happiness.

At the beginning of my senior year, Robert invited me to attend a campus gathering of the Fellowship of Christian Athletes.

"There is a lady named Corrie ten Boom who is going to speak. I would like you to come with me," he said.

I declined the invitation. Once again I realized this was for Christian people, and Jewish people just don't attend gentile religious gatherings. At least this was my thinking at the time.

Later, Robert told me what, Corrie ten Boom, said.

"You really missed it, Siegs," he said. "Corrie's family built a hiding place in their home during the Nazi occupation of Holland. A lot of Jewish people came to their home near Amsterdam, and they hid them in a special hiding place in the walls of their home. She would hide them and try to get them out of Nazi-occupied areas to safety. As a result, Corrie and her family got caught and were put into concentration camps. The majority of her family died in the concentration camps where they were sent. Corrie was also supposed to be executed, but a miracle happened, and she was released. She ended up traveling throughout the world, telling people about her faith in Jesus and her love for the Jewish people."

I thought to myself, *Why would someone want to risk their neck for a Jew? Whatever it means to be a believer, she is a real one. She is the real deal.*

I began to see the difference between true born-again Christians and people who might be just religious and hurtful toward Jewish people and others. I was told that Corrie shared about a personal relationship with God through Jesus when she was in prison with Jewish people and others. She led many to faith in Jesus during one of the most horrific times in history.

It was hard to get away from these thoughts. When I wanted a little bit better lunch I would go with my friend, Robert, to the training table. Guys on the football team who needed to keep up their weight had the opportunity to eat at the training table. During one of these lunches, my friend Robert asked me many questions.

"Do you believe in the Ten Commandments?"

"Yes, I do."

"Well, do you adhere to the Ten Commandments?"

"Well, they are hard to keep."

"So, what do the Jewish people do for forgiveness of their sins?"

"In the Jewish religion, there is a holiday called Yom Kippur," I told him. "It means Day of Atonement. On that day the high priest would take hold of a bull or a goat, shed its blood, and the blood would be the atonement for the people. This happened in the holy temple. Through this blood sacrifice, the people would be forgiven for their sins."

As I explained this, I realized there was no longer a temple in Jerusalem.

So I wondered, *What do we do now for forgiveness of sins?*

Robert told me, "Jesus was the atonement, the sacrifice for the Jewish people and for mankind. In Jeremiah 31:31 it says that God would have a new covenant with the house of Judah and the house of Israel. He would provide a new sacrifice."

Robert then said, "I'm a son of Abraham now, too." I said, "Of course you are. You are one of Ishmael's kids." Robert's grandmother was Syrian. He responded, "Although that is true, I am one of Abraham's children because of the promise that he was given by the Lord, that all the families of the earth would be blessed because of Abraham." He went on to say that this promise of the Savior of the Jewish and gentile people would come through Isaac, which included him.

Here was a gentile, whose ancestry was French, German, and Syrian, telling me what the Hebrew Scriptures meant. He said I needed Jesus, and His Holy Spirit, and repentance for forgiveness of my sins to be accepted into Heaven. I began to seriously question if I had lived the kind of life that would allow me to go to Heaven after I died. This is not the type of thing Jewish people usually discuss. We tend to believe that if we are good people, and do more good than evil, naturally God will grant us our rightful places in Heaven. Anyway, I had not really given it much thought before this, but now I found myself thinking about it over and over again.

One night before I went to bed in the fall of my senior year, I reflected back on my terrible junior year in baseball and what I had heard about Corrie ten Boom from my friend Robert.

I prayed a prayer that went like this: "God of Abraham, Isaac and Jacob, I don't exactly know who You are, but I know You say the Jewish people are your chosen people. I don't understand what we were chosen for. I truly don't know You, what Your thoughts are, what You look like, but here's my prayer. You know that in my sophomore year I had a great season. Last season I had a bad year and I was hurt. If You will restore my ability to pitch as I had in my sophomore year, then I will seek You further and begin my journey with You. If Jesus has something to do with this I don't know, but I will seek to know the truth about what I have been told. These born-again Christians seem to have a relationship with You that I long for, but don't have at this time. I pray, but You seem far off. I know that I am a sinner, but I do not know how to get rid of my sins. We no longer have the Holy Temple and there is no sacrifice on the holiday of Yom Kippur."

Senior Year Baseball

Baseball season began. My arm was back to full strength, and I was determined to finish strong my senior year. Despite my prayer, I was uncertain about how I would do. Our first spring training games were at Texas A & M University. I believe they were a nationally ranked team in the top twenty that year.

Coach Eilbracht penciled me in to start the second game of a doubleheader against Texas A&M. I knew he was giving me a shot to see if I could retain the stuff I had my sophomore year. Because they were such a good team, some of my teammates were concerned that we were in over our heads. The talk at our team meeting the night before was mostly negative, self-defeating chatter. But I believed we could win and said so to several of my teammates.

We won the second game 7-1. I had about seven strikeouts in that game and gave up seven hits. My fastball had totally regained its pop. That was my best pitch that day. My slider and curve were really working as well, yet I was a little wild, giving up about four walks. But I was really hard to hit that day. My ball was really moving. Now my record was 1-0. That was an incredible victory for our team and me. It was Texas A&M's second loss of the year bringing their season record to 20-2. Because of that game, I was scheduled to return to the starting rotation.

When the Big Ten season opened, I pitched against Northwestern University. Northwestern is in Evanston, Illinois, just a couple of miles north of the apartment where I grew up. So when I beat them, I got a conference win, which is a big deal. Many of my friends and family came to see me pitch that day. I had played American Legion baseball in summers previous with the Northwestern shortstop, Andy Spritzer. We beat Northwestern 8-2 that day as I pitched a complete seven-inning game.

I also pitched against the University of Minnesota, and Paul Molitor was their shortstop. He was being scouted heavily, and I was looking forward to pitching against him. In his first at bat, I threw a curve that broke sharply from his shoulders to his kneecaps. Paul had a spread stance and a compact swing. It seemed to me that as the ball approached, his eyes lit up like a pinball machine. The ball went into orbit. He had hit a home run off of me in his first at bat.

I made up my mind that I was not going to give him anything to hit in his next at bat. I threw a tight inside fastball, and he checked his swing, and the ball was caught up against the left field fence. This guy was the best I ever faced. I pitched well enough that day to be taken out with the game being close. We won the game 6-5. I pitched six innings and our relief pitcher, Tommy Stewart, came in and did a great job. We won the game in extra innings. I was not the winning pitcher, but it was an awesome experience to pitch against a future Hall of Fame player and national ranked team. Paul Molitor ended up getting over 3,000 hits in the major leagues.

At the end of my senior year at the University of Illinois, I was 4-0 and was going to pitch against Michigan State.

My roommate, Neal Siegel, went out for a run one day and came home and told me, "Jeff, I asked Jesus into my life and now I'm a completed Jew."

He said he read the Tanach (the Hebrews Scriptures) and realized that Jesus fulfilled all the prophecies of the Messiah. That absolutely blew my mind. Neal was someone I had a lot of respect for. He was now an engineering student and was playing in the University of Illinois Hockey Club.

"Neal, that's not for Jewish people!" I said. "That's for gentiles and now you're a Christian? You're not Jewish anymore."

"Just because I'm a Christian doesn't mean I stopped being Jewish," he replied. "The word *Christian* just means a follower of the Messiah. Jesus was a Jew. If you go and read the Hebrews Scriptures for yourself, you will find that all the prophecies and holidays predict the coming of the Jewish Messiah, who I have come to believe is Jesus. If you read it for yourself and hunger and thirst for righteousness, you will be filled. Jeff, I believe you will also come to the same conclusion I did."

A friend on the University of Illinois football team, named Jeffrey Goldberg, who was born Jewish, also made the same decision as Neal—to believe in Jesus. He actually made this decision before Neal did. This all began to impact me as I was beginning to see Jews believing in Jesus, and claiming to have never abandoned their Jewish faith.

The next time I saw my Grandpa Jack, I asked him, "Who do you think Jesus was?"

I had a lot of respect for him and valued his opinions.

"Jesus was a great prophet, a great rabbi, and a teacher of the Jewish people," my grandfather said. "He was a magician or a miracle worker like Moses."

Despite the persecution that Jewish people had suffered for centuries at the hands of people who called themselves Christians, my grandpa could not find any fault with Jesus. During that discussion with my grandfather, I felt like there was a sudden clarity in my understanding. I began to realize that I didn't find any fault with Jesus either. If my grandfather saw Jesus in a positive light while recognizing that Christians historically persecuted Jews, perhaps some of those who claimed to be His followers who hurt Jewish people were just impostors.

I read this verse later in Deuteronomy 18:15-19, "The Lord your God will raise up for you a Prophet like me from your midst, from your brethren. Him you shall you hear...I will raise up for them [the Jewish People] a Prophet like you [Moses] from among their brethren, and I will put my words in his mouth, and he shall speak to them all that I command Him. And it shall be that whoever will not hear my words, which he speaks in my name, I will require it of him" (NKJV).

I ended up my senior year with a record of 4-1 and a 3.19 ERA. I had just completed my undergraduate degree and a successful three-year stint on the baseball team. My overall win-loss record at the University of Illinois was 9-3, with a very good ERA.

****

2015 ILLINOIS BASEBALL PITCHING RECORDS

1. Kevin Duchene (2013-PRESENT) .2.39
2. Tom Stewart (1974-76) 2.51
3. Chuck Sommer (1972-73) 2.73
4. Dan Ingram (1974-76) 2.87
5. John Widdersheim (1977-78) 2.90
6. Josh Harshbarger (1977-78) 2.92
7. Jeff Innis (1981-83) 3.10
8. **Jeff Siegel (1974-76) 3.26**
9. Jeff Richards (1987-90) 3.40
10. Donn Pall (1983-85) 3.55

****

Chapter 6:

My Burning Bush Experience

After my senior year, I received a scholarship to go to graduate school. Coach Eilbracht awarded me a tuition scholarship to work on a Master's Degree in Physical Education. He asked me if I would become his assistant varsity coach and the junior varsity team's head coach. I had a full scholarship with a paying job!

From the outside, it appeared that I was on top of the world, but in reality, this was a time of great turmoil and great questioning. I had not forgotten what I had promised God before my senior baseball season that if He gave me my abilities back, I would seek Him and honor Him. Did a loving God really restore the abilities of a guy who was once a good pitcher to fulfill His divine purposes? I believed that He had kept His end of the bargain, that He had answered my prayer. Now, I would have to keep my word.

I borrowed a *Tanach* (the first five books of the Hebrews Scriptures also known as the Pentateuch) and the rest of the Hebrew Scriptures that were given to my brother, Bruce, for his Bar Mitzvah. I also had a Christian Bible called *The Way* that had the Bible prophecies Jesus had fulfilled highlighted in red letters. I was not interested in reading the New Testament yet.

At the time, I was living in an apartment complex not far from the fraternity house. I needed time away from my Jewish friends as well as my Christian friends in order to sort out some important issues. One day, I went into my bedroom, locked the door, and I took my brother's Hebrews Scriptures, held it up to heaven, and asked God two questions. I wanted God to speak to me in such a way that I would know my life's purpose.

"Who are you?" I prayed. And then I asked God, "Can I have a burning bush experience like Moses?"

I wanted God to speak to me in such a way that I would know my life's purpose. Could God show me how to find peace inside myself?

"Could You reveal those things to me?" I asked God. "Did You have a Son? I have to know if your Son was Jesus. And, is the answer to my burning bush experience somehow wrapped up in Jesus being the Jewish Messiah?"

I opened the Hebrew Scriptures, and I continued to pray to God, "Where do I begin my journey?"

I thought, *Why not with the first page.* I turned to Genesis chapter 1, verse 1, and read: "In the beginning, God created the heavens and the earth." The word for *God* in Hebrew is *Elohim.* The ending, *im,* on any Hebrew word tends to make that word plural. In the beginning God, *plural,* created the heavens and the earth. All of a sudden, it was as if scales were beginning to fall off of my understanding.

One God, Triune in Nature

I knew my friends Neal and Robert were very sincere and seemed to believe in the God of Abraham, Isaac, and Jacob. The problem I had with Christians was this. I explained to my born-again friends, "I believe in only one God. You say that you believe in one God, but you also say that you believe in God, Jesus, and the Holy Spirit. I count three gods." But Neal would say, "No, this is the Trinity. There is one God, but He is triune in nature."

So I asked God, "Can there be one true God who operates as a complex unity?"

In Genesis 1:26, God said, "Let us create man in our image." Now in my thinking, one God would say, "Let me create man in my image." Singular entity! But that's not how it's written. Now the "us" and the "our" are referring to God, and He is helping Himself create man. Yet, He is the only one creating.

Now somebody might say He was referring to angels, but He said, "Let us create man in our image." The only one created in the image of God is man. So, who was with God that is man-like and God-like at the same time? It could not be an angel, because an angel is never referred to as being in the image of God.

I didn't really understand what I was discovering, but I did realize that this one God had some kind of plurality. I continued in Genesis, coming upon a passage that suddenly had a whole new meaning. In Genesis 18, it says the Lord appeared to Abraham as he sat in his tent door one day. Abraham saw three men. When he saw them, he bowed down and said, "My Lord." He used the word *Adonai,* the word for the "Lord God." There were three men, and the Lord was one of those three men.

I had never realized before that the Lord God appeared to Abraham in the form of a man. Abraham actually had lunch with the Lord. He is eating with a man in a body of flesh who is God. *Adonai!*

I had to ask myself: "Who was Abraham eating with? Does this man have a name? What did Abraham and the Lord discuss over lunch?"

The concept of the Lord God appearing and not just speaking is incredible. I did not remember being taught this in Hebrew school, and I do not believe most Jewish people are taught on this subject. However, there it is plain as day, in one of the most important books of the Hebrew Scriptures. I was also reading in *The Way* Bible the references to many other passages in the Hebrew Scriptures that predicted the coming of the Messiah, where He would be born, His tribal lineage, as well as the time period in which He would be born.

In Genesis 32:1-32, Jacob wrestles with a man who changes his name to Israel. This encounter was so powerful that he calls the name of the place Peniel and says, "I have seen God face to face and my life is preserved." Who is this man that came in a body of flesh to wrestle and change Jacob's name? Can God inhabit human flesh?

Jeremiah 31:31 reads, "Behold the days are coming, says the Lord, when I will make a new covenant with the house of Israel and with the house of Judah, not according to the covenant that I had made with their fathers in the day that I took them by the hand to lead them out of the land of Egypt, my covenant which they broke, though I was a husband to them says the Lord. But this is the covenant that I will make with the house of Israel after those days, says the Lord. I will put my law in their minds, and write them on their hearts, and I will be their God and they will be my people. No more shall every man teach his neighbor, and every man his brother saying, know the Lord, for they shall all know me from the least of them to the greatest of them says the Lord. For I will forgive **their** [the Jewish people's] iniquity and remember **their** [the Jewish people's] sin no more" (emphasis added).

This covenant is for Israel and Judah. It is referring to a new agreement that is coming for the Jewish people. A day is coming in the future when all the Jewish people, from the least to the greatest, will know the Lord. I began to read Isaiah 52:13-15 and Isaiah 53:1-12 and these verses spoke of a servant who would be a sin offering for mankind and would give up his life for sin. It said this over seven times.

I asked myself, *Who could this be speaking about?*

I decided I needed some more answers. I went to speak with Cantor Philip Silverstein of my synagogue who actually lived, at that time, directly under our flat with his family. A cantor is similar to a worship leader in church, but has additional theological training. Cantor Silverstein was a very knowledgeable person in the Torah and the Prophets, and I respected his opinions. I wanted to hear his explanations of biblical passages, which I had read, especially Isaiah 53.

"Israel is the suffering servant," the Cantor told me. "They were the ones who suffered."

I did not argue with him, but I later went back and read the verses myself. Isaiah 53:4-6 says: "Surely he has borne our griefs and carried our sorrows. Yet we esteemed him stricken, smitten by God, and afflicted. But he was wounded for our transgressions. He was bruised for our iniquities. The chastisement for our peace was upon Him. And by his stripes we are healed. **All** [both Jews and gentiles] we like sheep have gone astray. We have turned **everyone** [Jews and gentiles] to his own way. And the Lord has laid on Him the iniquity of us all" (emphasis) added.

This was clearly about a *person*, not a nation. If the Jewish people are included "in all have gone astray," then *people* who *need* a sin offering cannot *be* the offering. This offering must be without spot or blemish. The only one without spot or blemish (perfect) is God Himself. He is the only one who could be this offering. I realized that the Jewish people may have suffered at times for righteousness sake, but at other times they suffered for their sins. Thus, the Jewish people are sinners, as are all human beings.

The Jewish high priest made an offering once a year on the Day of Atonement for himself, his family, and the nation. So, how could a people who needed a sin offering also be a sin offering? This is not possible nor could it be the context of these verses.

Isaiah 53: 8-11 says: "For the transgressions of my people He was stricken ... Yet it pleased the Lord to bruise Him. He has put Him to grief. When you make His soul an offering for sin ... By His knowledge My Righteous Servant shall justify many, for He shall bear their iniquities."

"Who is this servant?" I questioned. He had to be perfect and yet the only one who is perfect is God. How could God offer Himself as a sacrifice for sin if He is a spirit being? I realized the one who appeared to Abraham and had eaten lunch with him was the Lord who can inhabit a body of flesh if He wanted. And He did.

So God coming in the form of His Son, Jesus the Messiah, was now not only a possibility, but a reality!

My Burning Bush Experience!

As I prayerfully read the Hebrew Scriptures, I came to believe that Jesus was the Promised Jewish Messiah and Savior of all human beings. This was my **Burning Bush Experience.** I put the Bible on my bed and I fell on my knees. I looked up to heaven and prayed:

"Dear God, please come into my heart. I know that Jesus and God are one and the same. Please forgive me of my sins, for they are many. Please fill me with your Holy Spirit and lead and guide my life."

On October 29, 1976, I gave my life to Jesus (or in the Hebrew context *Yeshua*).

When I was done praying, I had an incredible feeling inside and a lot of questions:

Where do I go from here?

What are my next steps?

How is my family going to react?

A week later, my long-time friend, Neal Siegel, who was living in Michigan at the time, came down to baptize me. I realized that I would give Neal the honor of baptizing me, as he was an example of a Jewish believer in Jesus. Also, my friends from the Fellowship of Christian Athletes came to my baptism at a lake in Champaign, Illinois.

It was not long after I realized that I needed to call my dad. The Scriptures told me,

> *If you declare with your mouth, "Jesus is Lord," and believe in your heart that God raised him from the dead, you will be saved. For it is with your heart that you believe and are justified, and it is with your mouth that you profess your faith and are saved. As Scripture says, "Anyone who believes in him will never be put to shame. For there is no difference between Jew and Gentile—the same Lord is Lord of all and richly blesses all who call on him, for, "Everyone who calls on the name of the Lord will be saved." (Romans 10:9-13 NIV)*

I was anxious about how my dad would respond. Nonetheless, I had to make the call!

Chapter 7:

A New Life Begins

———————◆———————

"Hi, Dad," I said as I tried to sound calm and just normal, but to be honest my adrenalin was running high.

"Hello, Jeff, how are you doing?"

"Dad, I wanted to tell you that I have been reading the Hebrew Scriptures."

"Really?"

"Yeah, Dad, and after reading them, I did a careful study. After my examination I have come to the conclusion that Jesus is the Jewish Messiah, and I have made Him Lord of my life."

Silence you could have cut with a knife. I didn't know what else to say at this point.

Finally, in a stunned voice he asked, "But were you baptized?"

"Yes," I answered, simply but confidently.

I knew the impact would be great. I supposed his blood pressure would go through the roof, but I was not prepared for what he said next.

"You are worse than Adolf Hitler for what you have done, and you are a traitor to the Jewish people. You are not a Jew in my eyes and no longer welcome in my home. You are no longer my son." His voice cracked as he finished, "You are dead in my eyes."

For the first time in my life, I heard my dad cry. The phone went dead. I stared at the receiver in my hand and realized I had lost my dad. As hard as it was to receive, I did, however, realize that my dad's reaction was similar to that of other Jewish parents whose children had come to believe that Jesus is the Messiah. I knew that his mind had gone back hundreds of years to when the church became a political institution and began to force Jewish people at the edge of a sword to be baptized or give up their lives. It is unfortunate that over the centuries that what has called itself the church has not been a true example of God's love.

My salvation experience occurred at a unique juncture in history. There were not that many Jewish believers at the time I was saved, not many Messianic congregations locally or worldwide. I knew I was not going to be popular with my family or friends, but I had no idea I was going to lose my father. Despite his faults, he had always been an example to me. He was someone I looked up to, the one who taught me how to play the game that meant so much to me.

My mother was also very upset by my decision. I spoke with her not long after my call to my dad. She was embarrassed and worried what all her Jewish friends would think—the neighbors, cantor, rabbi, and synagogue members. Yet, my mom still loved me and was not about to disown her own son. I was only twenty-one years old at the time.

To become a follower of Jesus was a momentous decision for a Jewish person. Overall, I was considered a good guy, easy to get along with, and fun-loving. But now I had given my life to Jesus, and I became the black sheep of my family. At the university, I went from being a popular guy, a successful baseball player, to something of a pariah. The word spread among the Jewish fraternity houses that Jeff Siegel had gone crazy because he believes in Jesus. It was a very awkward time for me. If I called one of my friends, I might get a quick brush-off or no return call. I realized that by giving my life to Jesus, I was not only giving up my family, but many of my friends as well.

I looked again to Neal. Neal was very happy for me as he now had one of his best childhood friends to affirm his walk with Jesus. We had a long talk. I asked him what had happened to him after he became a believer in Jesus. He explained to me that his parents thought he had gone crazy. They wanted him to see rabbis and psychiatrists, but Neal hung in there. He was convinced in his heart of his faith in Jesus, yet he actually went to the rabbi out of respect for his parents. He had a respectful exchange with his rabbi. The rabbi concluded that Neal was sincere and explained to Neal's parents that he had a sound basis for his belief in Jesus and that being Jewish continued to be important to him.

During the mid-'70s, Jerry Gibson, a pastor of Webber Street Church of Christ and sponsor of the FCA campus chapter, was instrumental in helping facilitate many athletes and non-athletes coming to Jesus

He was a good example to me of someone who demonstrated patience in walking with the Lord, someone who had withstood opposition to his faith.

on the University of Illinois campus. Athletes would meet together for Bible study. In the fall of 1976, Robert Cline, and his brother, David, Stanley Stone, and one of Robert's friends on the football team, Bill Smith, started a Christian Bible study at the Jewish fraternity house.

Robert had been my friend and teammate for a while. He was a gifted athlete, who also possessed a bright mind and a charismatic personality. By now, he had been drafted to play professional football with the Cleveland Browns. In training camp in one of Cleveland's pre-season games, Robert sustained a bad knee injury. He was out for the season. He had signed a two-year contract and now came back for physical therapy to rehab his knee. He was tall, strong, and good-looking. He had a wide circle of admirers. If he made you his friend, you certainly felt privileged to be in that position. I began to attend the Bible study. It helped fulfill some of the loneliness of losing my family and some friends.

A Change in Lifestyle

I was walking away from a sinful lifestyle that was prevalent on campus and almost universally accepted. I was walking away from an unending string of parties, with abundant liquor flowing and sexual relations with no accountability or restraint. The Bible says that for a season sin is enjoyable. If a person has many sexual relationships, you leave a part of yourself with each person you are with, and that person with you. Unless you come to know the Lord, that brokenness becomes a part of your life and will stay with you the rest of your life outside of the Lord's forgiveness and healing power.

I wanted to walk with the Lord, but it was awkward for me to begin attending church. I had never attended a Christian service in a church. I had been to FCA meetings on campus, and to weddings in churches, but never to a worship service.

Spring of 1977 came, and I was a teacher in the College of Physical Education at the University of Illinois. I taught subjects like tennis, bowling, and electives that students could take for enjoyment and receive credit towards graduation. Those were the days of my little white tennis shorts, long wavy dark brown hair, and a mustache. I began to think about my future, yet it was still a confusing time for me as I was now without my Jewish family.

One of the students in my tennis class was a friend, Cheryl. She was Jewish and had a sister named Shelly. Cheryl was olive-skinned with dark brown hair and quite attractive. Shelly was younger and dated my friend, David Cline, who came to faith in Jesus before me. David had led Shelly to a relationship with Jesus.

Cheryl knew I had become a believer a few months before and mentioned to me that her sister Shelly now believed in Jesus.

She said, "Jeff, Shelly said that David speaks in a language called tongues and she has heard him do this. According to Shelly, only people close to God can do this. If David will come over and speak to me in tongues, I will believe in Jesus, too."

As a young believer, this caught me by surprise. This moment was like an oasis in my relationship desert. I told Cheryl I would call David and see if he could come over and speak to her in tongues.

When I called David he laughed and said, "I cannot come over and put on a spiritual freak show for Cheryl, but let me call a few friends from the Fellowship of Christian Athletes, and we will see what the Lord will do."

David came over to my apartment with some friends and Cheryl came as well. They asked me if they could have a time to pray with us and see what the Lord would do. We both said sure.

Our friends began to pray and the next thing I knew David was speaking in fluent Hebrew. I knew enough Hebrew from my five years of preparation for my Bar Mitzvah to know that this was what David was speaking.

Then someone from the group interpreted the Hebrew and said to me, "My son, the son of Abraham, Isaac, and Jacob, go to your people and tell them that the Messiah has come and will come back soon. You have no father here on earth; I am your father and will be faithful and watch over you."

I was not fluent in Hebrew, but knew enough words to know that I was being directly spoken to. I knew that David and the interpreter did not have the ability in themselves to do this. In a sense, this was like my second burning bush experience. The first was reading the Hebrew Scriptures and the Lord revealing to me that Jesus was Lord and Messiah.

Now the Lord was telling me, "This is your purpose in life, to go to your people (the Jewish people) and tell them the Messiah has already been here."

Cheryl and I had heard the same thing. It was obvious to me that we had experienced the supernatural power of God. Yet Cheryl chose to reject what she heard. She said that she thought David was speaking in Latin. The funniest part of all of this is that David was a Jersey boy and could only speak Jersey English. So, this is a little ironic, yet not surprising. Cheryl was a secular Jew without a Hebrew school education, like many in our culture.

Cheryl's parents were very concerned about what had happened to their daughter, Shelly, and asked both David and I if we would meet with them at their home in a northern suburb of Chicago. One would think that this was a great opportunity, but remember my dad had just kicked me out of my home only months earlier, and my mom and brothers were very embarrassed by my decision. I was not exactly the poster child of the Jewish community.

I also realized that to go and speak with Cheryl and Shelley's parents was not going to be easy. David and I asked all of our friends for prayer as we felt like we were being sent to a firing squad and this was like our last meal.

We took courage and asked the Lord for boldness and to touch us and equip us with His Holy Spirit.

When we spoke with them, I felt so new at all of this. I shared with them from the Bible why I made my decision to follow Jesus and David did as well.

They were polite and finished the meeting by saying, "Those are your decisions, but this is not for us or for our daughter."

They discouraged the relationship between David and Shelly. Eventually, they broke up and Shelly fell away from the Lord.

Even though I was a grad student living outside the fraternity house, I was still a member of Tau Epsilon Phi. Being a fraternity member implied a lifelong affiliation and I still had friends in the house and on campus. When my roommate, Steve Shapiro, nicknamed Schmoos, realized that I now believed in Jesus, he said that one of us needed to move out of the apartment. Through a miracle, I was offered a room back in the fraternity house.

I had come to faith, but I still had one foot in the world. I still went to bars with my friends and went out dancing. I retained many of my unbelieving friends from the baseball team. Besides the Bible studies at the fraternity house, one thing that was helping me to work my way away from sinful habits and more toward the Lord was a former Olympic gymnast.

Nancy was a sorority girl who happened to be very gorgeous. She and I really hit it off. She was a believer in Jesus. This was the first girlfriend with whom I could have Christian fellowship. She encouraged me in my faith in many ways. Her family attended a church in town. Nancy and I dated for about five months. We attended some of the Bible studies that were held in my fraternity house. I believe that Nancy was uncomfortable because of some of the things that members of this group were doing at that time such as preaching in public on campus.

Looking back I see that the method of the preaching was excessively harsh and not done in love. I believe that because Nancy was from a good Christian family, she picked up on this and was afraid that I was going to get mixed up with these Christians who were harsh in their delivery. She began to see their negative influence on me.

David and Robert began to publicly preach outside the campus Student Union building. At the rear entrance students hung out on a patio area. This was on the north end of the Quad, the main grassy area of the campus where thousands of students come and go, especially between classes. When Robert and David preached, they often preached on the judgment of God. They preached a harsh gospel that God was going to come and judge this nation for abortion and other things like that. Some young people were attracted to that message. Robert actually led quite a few people to Jesus through his messages.

I also preached on the Quad, near the Student Union. It was an awkward experience for me and not natural, but I felt it was an opportunity to preach the gospel to reach my peers. Robert and David were examples to me, like John the Baptist, giving warnings to our generation. Our essential message was, "Prepare for the coming of the Lord; those who aren't prepared will experience God's judgment." We were all preaching the message, "As it was in the days of Noah, so would be the coming of the Lord. People would be eating, drinking, making merry, and caught unaware by the flood." We had some of the truth, but it was delivered in a harsh manner. The fact that I was part of a well-known group who preached in public and a laughingstock to many students really embarrassed Nancy.

"I don't picture myself preaching like that," she told me one day. "This brand of Christianity is not for me."

That summer, Nancy was offered a job as a television commentator for NBC Sports. About that time, we broke up. It was clear to me that our different views on what it meant to be a Christian had something to do with our breakup. The only form of Christianity I knew at that time was from those guys. They were my closest friends. Nancy could tell there was harshness in my spirit and she attributed this to my friendships in the Bible study.

This sweet, intelligent, Christian girl suddenly wanted nothing to do with me and that should have been a warning. She understood what a genuine Christian was, but had no respect for the people with whom I was associating. I should have paid better attention to what she shared with me.

During this time, my mother had talked my father into letting me back into their home, but I was not welcomed back by my father with open arms. It was a very tense environment. It was more of a reluctant type of thing on his part, something forced on him by my mom and grandparents. My father was a very stubborn, harsh man.

One day, I was talking to my grandfather about my decision to believe in Jesus, and my father exploded.

"Who do you think you are bringing the name of Jesus into this home?" he yelled. "Do you think anyone here wants to hear about Jesus Christ, the enemy of our people?"

I thought he might slug me. That kind of explosion embarrassed my mother, who was a kind, gentle person. That made it even tougher on me, seeing my mother so uncomfortable because of my father's reactions. My mother was also concerned that I might bring shame to the family by letting neighbors in on the news that I was a Christian.

"While you are here, please don't talk about Jesus with the cantor," she implored. "If you bump into the rabbi's children, promise me you won't talk about Jesus."

Then my brother, Rick, a junior at the University of Illinois, would chime in, "It really embarrasses me when some of your friends are out preaching on the Quad."

Rick now lived in the same fraternity house. He kind of liked Robert Cline and didn't mind when he became a Christian, but it really bothered him when I followed suit. Years later he told me that he realized how much he loved me when he felt he had lost me. It truly hurt him. He wanted the old Jeff back.

So, by spending time with my family, I was actually becoming more alienated from them than when I was staying away. I especially missed my father, who had gone from being a mentor to me in some ways to becoming a kind of adversary. Before, despite his harsh exterior, I could always turn to him for counsel regarding decisions. Now, there was no way I could bring anything to him for discussion. When I came to Jesus, I saw the worst in my father.

I was alienated and afraid to come home; it had become an unpleasant place to be. I was also immature and did not know how to temper my belief in Jesus and walk softly in front of my father. I also doubted if my dad even loved me. I could not understand how a father could kick his child out of the family without trying to understand why I had made this decision. Losing a father figure was very tough on me. It was tearing me up inside, because I did not know how to cope with the feeling of loss, which was akin to grief.

Not long after that, I went to the Hillel Foundation in Champaign and met with Rabbi Steinberg, a campus rabbi. I was having some doubts about my decision. I felt so alone. I was just getting pounded with rejection and fears of loneliness. I met him in his office. He was in his thirties at the time, casual clothes, and this made it comfortable to speak with him. He seemed to be a gentle, kind person.

"Can you prove to me through the Torah that Jesus is not the Messiah," I said to Rabbi Steinberg.

Rabbi Steinberg.

"Jeff, I can't do that," he said.

"Why can't you?" I shot back. "You don't believe in Jesus, do you?

"Just as there are many roads leading into Champaign-Urbana, who am I to say that there aren't many roads leading into Heaven," he said.

I came to the rabbi to see if he could shake my faith, but now it seemed more like I was shaking his through the process of our conversation.

This was not my intention. I shared with him about my experiences, and he appeared somewhat stunned by the things I was telling him. Instead of presenting me with evidence that the Messiah could not be Jesus, he helped confirm to me that the decision I had made was right and that the facts were in the Hebrew Scriptures.

I felt that God was encouraging me to not be afraid of sharing my belief and my testimony.

Fight the good fight of faith. Take hold of the eternal life to which you were called when you made your good confession in the presence of many witnesses. (1 Timothy 6:12 NIV)

Chapter 8:

Following the Fellowship

In the winter of 1977, Robert Cline, had rehabbed his knee and was on his way to the spring training camp with the Cleveland Browns. Before he headed out, he and his brother, David, broke away from the Fellowship of Christian Athletes and started a church with no name. They had already begun to pull away from traditional churches. There were three elders of this church.

As it turned out, Robert's time with the Cleveland Browns was short lived. He flunked his preseason physical and immediately returned to Urbana. Upon his return he, too, was appointed an elder by the other elders.

The reason the church didn't have a name is because the leaders of the group thought that in the Bible a church just took on the name of the city where they met. They wanted the group to have the same closeness as the people in the Book of Acts, in which they broke bread together often, and even held all things they owned in common. Most of the time, we referred to the church as the Fellowship.

There were a few older couples involved with the church as well. Toby and Rita Kahr were in their late forties and enjoyed the zeal of our desire to take the Bible at face value. Toby was the Director of Human Resources at the University of Illinois, and he had invited me to his home on a few occasions. He was a Jewish believer in Jesus and was very understanding about the loss of my family due to my faith in Jesus.

He and Rita would become two of my closest friends, instrumental in helping me through some of the darkest times of my life. Toby Kahr, became a spiritual father to me years later. Rita, a gentile believer, also had a great love for the Jewish people and became a Christian mother to me. Toby reached out to me and many of the young people who were becoming Christians at the University of Illinois. Toby could see some overzealousness of the leadership, but his attitude was that we were young. He felt with proper mentoring from older Christians, we would be fine.

Indeed, after several years, this fellowship of believers would move to a space in a church building in Urbana called, New Life Church. About fifty or sixty members, mostly young people, began meeting at New Life Church.

In the summer of 1978, I was working as an umpire for the Urbana Park District's slow pitch softball league.

After one of the games, one of the other umpires said, "Our score-keeper needs a ride home."

Her name was Terri Mellskog. Amazingly, in twin cities where nearly 100,000 people, besides students, called home, Terri lived right across the street from me. We both lived on Healy Avenue, one block off Green Street, the main drag of Campus Town, which was jammed with bars, restaurants, clubs, and shops that catered to students. We talked a little bit on the ride home and a little longer in my car.

It turned out that we were both studying physical education. I was a grad student, and she was about to begin her junior year. I suggested that one day we might go out for a run together.

Here is Terri's account of how we met:

I decided to stay on campus and get a job with the Urbana Park District the summer going into my junior year. One of my jobs was to supervise the adult softball league in the evenings. I was at a park, maybe Prairie or Woodlawn. I was to unlock the rest rooms, turn the lights on, and keep score. At the end of the night, I was to phone in the scores to the local newspaper, lock up everything, and go home. I usually got a ride home from a particular umpire because I didn't have a car and the buses stopped running that late at night.

One night, the umpire who usually gave me a ride home was going in the other direction. He asked another umpire, Jeff, if he would give me a ride home instead. When I told Jeff where I lived, we discovered I lived right across the street from him. We both lived a block off of Green Street, in the heart of Campus Town.

I recognized him, but I didn't know where I had seen him before. Then I remembered seeing him painting the hall one time. He was also the maintenance man for my apartment building.

When he went to drop me off, we sat in his car; and he began sharing his faith in Jesus with me. He explained that he was a Jewish believer and all that.

I thought, "Oh boy, I got a ride home with a Jesus freak."

But I'm a real polite person, so I just let him talk. He was good at talking. The more he talked, the more I had questions about what he was saying. I told him what I understood about what you need to go to Heaven.

"I'm a good person," I said. "And I grew up going to church with my parents."

"That is not what the scriptures say," he said. "You must confess that Jesus is Lord and that He died and rose from the dead for your sins. It is about the transformation of your heart and mind by faith. This is the gift of God."

"My grandmothers are believers and one has given me a Bible. They keep talking to me about Jesus."

The more he talked, the more I got concerned about my afterlife. I initially got saved because I wanted to save myself from Hell.

Then one day a few weeks later, he was across the street at his apartment barbecuing over a little hibachi. He called me over and asked me if I wanted something to eat. I told him I was fine. Then he took me back to his apartment and introduced me to his roommates, David Cline and John Scolito. Back outside I remembered where I had seen Jeff on campus. To me, he was a big man on campus. I used to see him on the Quad, with his letterman jacket on, hanging out with the other athletes. He was very popular. I was just an ordinary person. He was now in graduate school. So, it surprised me when he asked me out on a date.

I was like, "Are you sure you want to go out with me?"

"Yes, of course, I do," Jeff said.

"Okay, if you really want to."

Then he walked me back home. On our first date he took me to see the Disney movie, "The Jungle Book." Then, we went to Garcia's Pizza for dinner.

One day, I saw Terri across the street. I invited her over and then invited her into my apartment and introduced her to David. As we walked out of the apartment, I noticed that she had the most beautiful blue eyes.

The next thing I knew I was saying, "When are we going to get together?"

She laughed and said something like, "Yeah, right, you're just kidding."

"I'm serious, I would like to go out with you," I said.

About two weeks later, we went out on our first date to see the animated movie, *Jungle Book*. We went to the movie theater a few blocks away on Green Street. Afterwards we met some friends at Garcia's Pizza, a popular restaurant at that time. We both liked Garcia's Pizza. I walked her home and she invited me into her apartment.

I had told her about my faith in Jesus, so she pulled out a Bible one of her grandmothers had given to her. She said both of her grandmothers were Christians. All of her grandparents were Swedish. Her parents weren't born in Sweden, but her grandparents were. Terri explained to me that her grandmother, Alida Mellskog, was a Pentecostal Christian, who prayed for her every day.

As we said good night, Terri said, "I had a lot of fun. I would like to invite you over for dinner the next time."

That dinner date never materialized. On the weekend, we were supposed to get together. I called Terri repeatedly and knocked on her door. I even found her parents' phone number and called them, thinking maybe she was visiting them at their suburban Chicago home, but she was not there either. I realized that I was becoming very fond of Terri and was wondering if she had similar feelings for me.

I realized that dating was now different for me. Since I was now a Christian, I could no longer lead a promiscuous life. I was going to go and see Terri and be honest that I was developing feelings for her. I realized that it was more important to develop a friendship with her and pray for her relationship with Jesus.

When I went to see Terri, I explained that I thought that we were supposed to get together for her dinner engagement. This caught her by surprise. She felt that her original invitation was just an informal gesture and still did not believe that I had much interest in her. I explained my respect for her and that I desired to continue in friendship with her, but it appeared to me that she was not very interested. I headed toward the door.

As I began to walk out the door she said, "Please come back. I do want to go out with you."

From that time, Terri began to read the Bible that her grandmother had given her. Soon after, she invited Jesus in her heart and was saved. This was in 1978. I believe that she was baptized in the same lake that I was.

In the fall of 1978, I left graduate school when I was about two-thirds done and worked as a substitute teacher, hoping to get a foot in the door for a permanent teaching position as a gym teacher in Champaign or Urbana. I substituted in high schools in Urbana and middle schools in Champaign. My plan was to land a job and then go back and finish my Master's Degree in Physical Education.

I asked Terri if she would come with me to Chicago to meet my family and go dancing with us. This seemed like a good time to her and she said sure. When I took Terri up to Chicago to meet my parents, it was their anniversary. We all went to dinner at the restaurant on the 97th floor of the John Hancock building, the tallest building in the city at that time.

We had a nice time and my parents seemed to like Terri. It was not long after that I invited Terri to a Christian retreat at Ben Israel Ministries in Bemidji, Minnesota. We went with Robert, David, and other Christian friends. It was then that I realized how much I cared for Terri. We prayed together about our relationship and for the Lord's will.

I did not want this to be the same as in other relationships. I did not want to hurt Terri or to be hurt myself. Terri was also seeing another young man at the time. I encouraged her to date if she wanted.

I believed that if she was to be my sweetheart, the Lord would put this in her heart and she would want to be with me.

About a month after we returned from Ben Israel, Terri stopped seeing this other guy and confessed that she only wanted to see me.

I remember coming home and I prayed to God, "If you want Terri to be my wife, when I propose to her she will say *yes*."

My Proposal

After praying this prayer, Terri and I continued to date and fellowship together. In October 1978, after knowing Terri for about four months, I went to her apartment and she made dinner for me. I got on my knees, asked her if she would be the mother of my children, and if she would marry me. It was as if Terri was not surprised. She just smiled and we held each other.

I went to see my parents in Chicago with Terri to share our decision with them. They were beginning to like Terri. This was a miracle because when I was younger my dad used to threaten me to never marry a non-Jewish woman.

Terri was in the room at the time when I spoke to my dad. He wanted her to know he was unhappy with me, but not about our marriage.

"Jeff, I want you to know that Terri is not the problem here," he said. "You are! It's your being a Christian that is the problem. I accept Terri, but I will not be part of a church wedding. If you want your mother and me to be part of your wedding at all, I want you to go before a judge at the court house and have a legal wedding."

I was actually grateful that my dad tried to be a part of our wedding in some way. But I was disappointed at not being able to have what you would call a normal wedding with your parents celebrating with you.

Then we went to see Terri's parents about my proposal. Her father was a retired colonel in the Army National Guard who had a successful flooring business. Her mother worked in management for Marshall Field's. I had met her parents once or twice before this, and her mother had let Terri know she was not happy about her daughter dating a Jewish man.

She had once asked Terri, "This isn't serious, is it?"

As Terri was growing up, her mother intimidated her. Besides not liking Jewish people, her mother particularly did not care for Christians. She had mistreated her mother for being a Christian as well as her mother-in-law for the same reason.

Terri's parents were both anti-Semitic, but Terri didn't grow up feeling that way. Once when Terri was growing up, she heard her mother say, "They own everything." Terri couldn't understand why people were so upset with Jewish people. They're not in our prisons and not on our welfare rolls. They have made great movies, made great scientific discoveries; they are doctors; what is all the fuss about? Later, Terri heard her father had a bad experience with a Jewish business partner.

Terri's family was never close and they never talked about intimate things together. When Terri played sports in school, her parents never came to any of her games—not a swim meet, not a volleyball game, not a basketball game, not a softball game. When Terri dated in high school or college, they never took an interest in whom she was going out with.

So, here I was in the home of people who were very negative toward Christianity, but also disliked Jewish people. When I sat down with Terri's father on that winter night, I was very respectful toward him. I asked for his blessing on our marriage.

He seemed rather agreeable and said something like, "Well, we'll talk again."

The next time I went over to her parents' house, the tone had changed. Terri's mom began the conversation by saying to me, "How dare you go to my husband and ask for Terri's hand in marriage without including me?" I said that I had assumed that the proper thing to do would be to go to Don first and he would inform her of my intentions, then we would meet again, and I would as her as well. Her father started asking me questions.

"What are your plans about having children? Are you going to practice birth control?"

"We are going to live by faith," I told him.

"You are going to do what?" he said.

He freaked out. He thought we were pretty crazy. Of course, we ended up not doing that. We used appropriate birth control methods during the course of our marriage, but at that moment I was still young in my faith in Jesus. Terri's father had walked away from his faith in Christ as a young man and was intolerant of Christians. Instead of reaching out to me as a young believer and giving me some good advice, he pulled away.

Then Terri's dad asked us to wait until Terri graduated before we got married. Terri had one semester left at that time.

Her father said, "If you will allow my daughter to finish college, and allow her to work a year or two in a job, then we will think about giving you our blessing."

I felt that he was stalling for time and wanted to get rid of me so I asked, "Are you being sincere, that you would give us your blessing, or are you just trying to buy time?"

"We are hoping our daughter will see the light as she gets older," he said. "She is very young; too young to even consider marriage. You are older than she is and should understand this."

Terri was twenty-one years old at the time. I was twenty-three years old.

"I really don't know what to say to you," I said. "I feel that my being born Jewish has something to do with your feelings. I can't change that. If being a Christian offends you, I will not be changing that either. I don't think there is anything we could do to obtain your blessings."

We would have gladly waited out of respect for Terri's parents, if that would have meant that they would have given their blessing on our marriage. But her father's position was clear.

He stood up, finalizing the conversation, "You know what, just go and do what you're going to do."

After that Terri's parents were so dead set against our relationship that they would not even help her financially to finish college. After being estranged from my own family for believing in Jesus, I had thought perhaps I would find a sense of family with Terri's family. After all, they were gentile people who I thought normally embraced the Christian faith. Instead, I found myself rejected by her family also. Instead of me gaining a new mother and father, Terri lost both of her parents as well. The pain of being separated from both sets of parents was felt deeply by both of us.

Even Terri's grandmother, Alida, her father's mother, asked Terri to give back the engagement ring to me. Terri asked her grandmother why she felt that way and initially she said because I was Jewish. Terri's grandmother was a believer in Jesus and one given to much prayer. A few weeks later Terri's grandmother, Alida, called and asked to speak with Terri and me.

She said that she prayed to the Lord about our marriage and here is what the Lord said to her, "Alida, all these years you have asked for your grandchildren to come to Jesus and marry a good believer in the faith. Now I give you one of My Chosen People and you reject my provision for your granddaughter."

Terri's grandmother, Alida, asked us to forgive her for her mistake and we got along well from that time on.

Terri and I wanted a Christian wedding and for friends and family to be there. I decided to do whatever I could to honor my dad's wishes that I get married in a courthouse. We went to the courthouse in Urbana a few days before our Christian ceremony and were legally married with my parents in attendance.

Terri and I were married in the church on June 30, 1979. It was a joyous and a sad occasion all at the same time. My mother and father were not at our Christian wedding ceremony, and her parents did not make it to Champaign-Urbana for either of the ceremonies.

Our Wedding and Early Years of Marriage

Our wedding and small reception was at the Urbana Assembly of God. Toby Kahr agreed to be the Master of Ceremonies at our Christian wedding. One of the elders of our fellowship was touring with the singing group Petra, a nationally known Christian band and one of the pioneers of Christian contemporary music. He wrote some music for us and Petra played at our wedding. David Cline, as one of my best friends, led Terri to the altar.

While Terri's parents did not attend the wedding, her uncles, her grandmothers, and one of her sisters attended. In a lot of ways, it was awkward and strange, with her parents not there. Still, it was a beautiful wedding with many of our brothers and sisters in Christ from Champaign-Urbana attending.

In my vows, I said I did not have much more to give her than my love. I promised to be faithful to her and walk with the Lord the best way I knew how. Terri said similar things, but ended quoting from the book of Ruth, "Your God will be my God, and your people will be my people."

We didn't have much money for a proper honeymoon. A friend who had a small home in Southern Illinois offered it to us for a week. In addition to that, my dad bought us a room for a night at the Hyatt Regency in Chicago near O'Hare Airport.

After our honeymoon, Terri and I found a cute little starter home in the small town of Fithian, Illinois, about twenty-five miles from Urbana.

Our home was located on about a quarter acre of land with exceptionally fertile, black soil. Our neighbor, a railroad conductor and organic gardener, got permission from the railroad for Terri and me to use a plot of land near the railroad tracks to plant a large garden. We grew a lot of vegetables like tomatoes, corn, onions, broccoli, zucchini, etc. Terri enjoyed canning and we filled up our deep freezer for the winter. The black Illinois soil produced so many tomatoes that she canned more than enough to last the winter. Terri was finishing up college while I managed a Payless gas station in Danville, about a half hour east of Fithian. I was making pretty good money at the time.

I later got a better job at the University of Illinois with the Police Training Institute. Toby Kahr, who was the Director of Human Resources, helped me to obtain this position. My responsibilities were to manage classroom support for the instructors who trained cadets in the Police Academy.

Terri's parents had somewhat cut us off, and it was very hurtful. They did not acknowledge our marriage, and Terri's mom would encourage her to divorce me. I did not know why I was being treated with such cruelty. In the early days of our marriage, her mom would send Christmas gifts for our children and Terri, but there was no acknowledgment of our marriage. That was very painful. It was awkward to be invited to their home at Christmas, realizing they did not want me there. At these times, Terri's mom refused to speak with me or even acknowledge my presence.

Do not be anxious about anything, but in everything, by prayer and petition, present your requests to God.
(Philippians 4:6 NIV)

Chapter 9:

Losing Sight of Christ

In the summer of 1979, Terri and I were settled in our little starter home in Champaign-Urbana. We continued fellowship with the church that had no name. We were a group of believers in Jesus whose numbers had grown to around 125. People were getting saved, kicking all types of addictions, eating healthy, and starting to live their lives for Jesus. It was an exciting time. We were a very zealous group of young people who wanted to be followers of Jesus and live out our faith in a way that was meaningful, rather than just a Sunday religion. The problem was that it went to extremes. Youthful pride got out of control.

A turning point in the fellowship came when a preacher arrived from England. His name was Derek Gitsham. It was in the fall of 1979 that he brought with him some false doctrines, which our new leaders bought into hook, line, and sinker. He said the women had to wear cloth head coverings at all times to show they were submitted to their husbands and submitted to God.

He was misinterpreting a scripture, taking it out of context, and turning it into a new law for our church. Legalism of all kinds entered into our fellowship.

Toby Kahr sat down with the leaders and said, "The preaching from this man is wrong. The scripture he was referring to, 1 Corinthians 11:1-16, was not referring to a piece of cloth, but rather to a woman having long hair. Even if it were a cloth, it could have applied to the culture of the region at that time, rather than the establishment of a new law for all time."

Toby went on to say that more was at stake than just an interpretation of a scripture.

"I see more than a piece of cloth to be worn by women; I see a domination of people's faith. I see a false covering of man coming into the fellowship and you will be dominated by the leadership if you take on this belief," he warned them.

However, Robert insisted that the preacher from England was right, and women must wear head coverings in his fellowship. Toby's wife, Rita, was an outspoken woman, and she shared her thoughts also.

"I am not wearing any head covering," she said.

In response, the group's leaders Branded her a "Jezebel," insinuating she was a rebellious woman, dishonoring her husband and the Lord.

Toby told the leaders, "We are going to have to leave this fellowship. You are making a serious mistake here. My wife is not putting any cloth on her head."

I listened to the argument, but did not feel that I understood the Scriptures well enough to draw my own conclusion from the subject. Somehow, Robert's arguments were more convincing than Toby's to me. We had turned a corner. After that, it was clear to those on the outside that the leaders wanted more and more control over all the members.

Toby continued to warn me about the wrong direction the fellowship was going. He even wrote me a personal letter telling me about his love for all of us including Robert. He was broken hearted that he had to leave, but he knew that we had taken on false doctrine that the Apostle Paul warned of in Galatians 1:6-9.

> *I marvel that you are turning away so soon from Him who called you in the grace of Christ, to a different gospel, which is not another; but there are some who trouble you and want to pervert the gospel of Christ.* (NKJV)

Toby was trying to tell me I was being deceived to believe in another gospel. Not having any doctrinal background other than the understanding of how to be saved, I made a terrible decision. I didn't listen to Toby and other older people who felt the same way and began to leave the fellowship. I was a little distant from older Christians because of the loss of my parents and Terri's. I did not recognize at that time that God was giving Toby and Rita to Terri and me to replace the parents we lost for our belief in Jesus.

Instead, I proceeded to come under the teaching of Robert and the elders. I was getting in deeper and deeper. I was asked to be a deacon at the church in the late fall of 1979. The deacons did various tasks at the church, such as setting up chairs and organizational matters.

In the fall of 1980, four or five more families left the fellowship as they became uncomfortable with the leadership. There was a power struggle among the leaders in January 1981, with two of the elders stepping down as elders and leaving. Robert Cline was now the lone elder in the church. Little by little Robert was pushing out leaders who disagreed with him, and replacing them with others who would not challenge his decision-making or his preaching.

I didn't fully recognize this because the harshness that came through Robert also had come through my father and some of my coaches. It was easy to accept. I had not had an example of God's love in my home. I was brought up in an abusive spirit and was deceived into thinking that this was normal behavior. I was not ready to see the light that Toby and others tried so hard to reveal.

This was my first and only church experience. Robert also had a harsh attitude toward the other churches in the area. He pronounced judgments on the churches in town and began to pray for them as if they had fallen away.

"The other pastors are Pharisees," he would preach. "They are compromisers of the faith and God will judge them."

We did not walk in unity with any other church in Champaign-Urbana. Robert and the new leadership he was setting up to replace the ones who were leaving created their own system of accountability among themselves. All outside Christian input was being driven away. I did not have a firm grip on good doctrine. I was not aware at the time that young men in the faith and ministry should have older, godly mentors.

This is something that this young leadership did not have. Not one of our leaders had any education outside of a secular bachelor's degree. They did not have the tools to stay on the right

These mentors are so important because older Christian men are more likely to be grounded in good theology, solid doctrine, and life experience.

path because not one of them had a Bible school degree nor had served in any ministry apprenticeship to gain the experience needed to be able to see the pitfalls of false doctrine. No one should come into eldership without first being tested by coming under the direction and wisdom of older men who have years of Christian leadership. You can see in the Bible how Paul mentored Timothy and Titus. John Mark was mentored by Paul and later by Barnabas.

1 Timothy 3:6-7 talks about young men coming into leadership too soon lest they become conceited and fall into Satan's trap.

Robert and the leadership were now out of control. Robert was beginning to move in the direction of a self-pronounced apostle. I remember long morning, prayer meetings and prophesy about God's judgment on our nation, the church, and local churches. Robert began to pray loudly for people by name in a judgmental manner. We all joined in and followed suit.

Various students in our church were getting ready to graduate. They wanted to get good jobs in other cities and get on with their lives. Robert would either prophesy over them with a word not to leave, or just tell them if they left that they were in disobedience to the Lord. The further insinuation was that if you disobeyed a prophetic word that Robert gave, you were in rebellion to the Lord. This was manipulation, but I did not realize it at the time. He was setting himself up as God's prophet and those under him as other prophets and apostles.

Furthermore, Robert surrounded himself with "yes men" and would not listen to any counsel from outside his group of self-appointed leaders. If we disagreed with him, he told us we were self-righteous. Robert used scriptures like 2 Chronicles 20:20 to say, "Obey God's prophets and so you will prosper." Of course, that meant he was God's prophet and we needed to listen to him. His insinuation was that he was a prophet. He had all the truth. He was in charge, and nobody else was going to tell him anything.

When his brother, David, disagreed with him, he got the self-righteous and rebellious lecture from Robert. David always looked up to Robert because he was a superstar athlete, an All Big Ten in baseball, and had signed a two-year contract to play with the Cleveland Browns. Whenever David disagreed with Robert, he laid a guilt trip on him and

David just knuckled under. David was coming more and more under his big brother's influence.

Early in 1981, Robert appointed David, Jim Manly, Robert Cary, and me as elders. A church began in Clifton, New Jersey, as a result of Robert's frequent visits home in 1981. Robert and David were from Clifton and their grandmother had a very large home that was left to them after her death. They started a church in that home. They had about fifty members. David Cline and Jim Manly prepared to move to Clifton to lead that group.

Melissa, our first child, had just been born April 8, 1981, and I was still working at the Police Training Institute. It was a big honor for me at the time to be asked to be an elder of the church. I was like an assistant pastor. Terri and I wanted to get closer to my new job and responsibilities in the Fellowship. I moved my family to an apartment complex in Urbana called Willow Brook on the north end of town where many group members and some of the leaders lived. Terri was given some light management responsibilities in return for free rent. Terri did not have to work outside the home and therefore had more time for Melissa. With free rent, my monthly salary of about $1,000 plus benefits seemed like a lot of money at the time.

When Robert taught the Bible, he could go on for hours. People would listen to him, and he would hold our attention. We thought he was a good Bible teacher. I was an understudy to Robert, but I was emulating someone who was exerting his own authority in an extremely negative way. I was being taken unknowingly further and further away from God.

Looking back at it now, it seems that he had the same personality as many of the worst dictators the world has known, many of whom loved to speak for hours at a time to captive audiences like Adolf Hitler, Fidel Castro, and others. They seemed sincere at first, but a time came when they attained a level of power that could no longer be questioned as they now led through fear. In a sense, they became like God to their listeners.

I came to accept Robert as a Moses figure in my life. People in the group would prophesy over him, encouraging him to lead God's people like Moses did in the Bible. Robert pretended he did not like the fuss, but he actually encouraged it. I am ashamed to say that I became one of those people who played into this deception. I was now totally under Robert's influence.

I believe my marriage was suffering from my passion to be a good leader in the group, and especially because of my intense loyalty to Robert. As I became more involved with the group, my marriage was losing its closeness. Terri liked to do things together as a family, like educational and fun outings, but I did not dedicate as much time for those things anymore.

Humility Was Conspicuously Absent

With the zeal of those who believed fervently, we preached that others should follow us as we followed Christ. Humility was conspicuously absent because we felt we knew much more than anyone else. However, we were not really following Christ at all; we were following a man who liked to be followed. We were the "prophets." I was becoming a Robert Cline clone. I believed that he was serving God, and if I wanted to become more Christ-like, I would become more like him.

In 1 Corinthians 11:1 Paul wrote, "Imitate me, just as I also imitate Christ." To me, Robert was the demonstration of what a man of God was like in the same way that Paul showed forth the likeness of Christ to people of his age. Of course, there was an enormous difference. Paul was a humble man who had spent years in the wilderness getting to know God and being mentored by Barnabas and others in the church before starting his ministry. Paul then met with Peter and the Apostles in Jerusalem, who had been with Jesus three years, to make sure that he had a clear understanding of his own preaching and teaching of the life of the gospel of Jesus Christ. Paul's example of humility was that he went all the way to Jerusalem to make sure that he was preaching the gospel of Christ properly among the gentiles.

Robert was a proud man who believed in himself, but was not really showing the attributes of the loving Christ. I also became a proud man. I looked up to Robert. I wanted to dress like

The Apostle Paul willingly submitted himself to others, was willing to be wrong, and be adjusted by others who had actually walked personally with Jesus.

the guy, wanted to eat like the guy. I wanted to speak loudly like him; I wanted to pray like him. I wanted to be self-disciplined like him. If he got a Toyota Corolla, I wanted to have one, too. If Robert had it, obviously it was the best. All of Robert's followers wanted to be just like him as well. He claimed to be like the Apostle Paul.

"Imitate me," he said.

So that's what I and others did. He said he didn't have a bank account but paid everything in cash. So that is what we did, too. If he donated twenty percent of his income to the church, I was doing the same thing. If Robert proclaimed that white flour or white sugar were bad for your health, people would take that as the law to live by. If they wanted to use any foods that he did not recommend, they had better not tell anyone else in the group about it. Please understand that eating healthy is a great thing, but each person has to be motivated out of his own freewill without any subtle manipulation. Within the group, everybody was expected to do what Robert wanted them to do.

Some things were subtly required and other things were more clearly mandated. People became very legalistic and started to take on the harsh and controlling attitudes that accompany legalism. The situation was now out of control and getting worse.

By following Robert and imitating him, I lost sight of Christ. Of course, I did not know that at the time. Eventually, I also lost my identity as a Jew. I lost my identity as an athlete. I lost my identity as a believer in Jesus. Instead, I became a religious fanatic. We all became cookie-cutter religious weirdoes. This was my own fault and it would not be long before I had to take full responsibility for these wrong decisions.

Pride Goes Before Destruction

This abuse of authority soon resulted in mental and physical abuse of group members that became a regular part of the group. I became subject to Robert. My wife became subject to me. I was under Robert's thumb. My wife was under my thumb. At any time, he could give me a "prophetic word," telling me I had committed some kind of sin against God or the group. I wanted to avoid this. I wanted to stay in his favor. Since I was his clone, I was also giving "prophetic words" to others, abusing my authority in the same way that he was.

Shortly after I became an elder, Robert went to preach in Spokane, Washington, in early 1982. As a result, the church he preached at split in two. He became the leader of the new church and decided to move to Spokane. His brother, David, came back from New Jersey to lead the church in Champaign-Urbana.

I was asked to co-pastor the church with David and later become the pastor in Champaign-Urbana so David could go back to New Jersey. I now left my good job at the Police Training Institute for a faith-based ministry. The church did not pay me a salary. We had an offering box at the rear of the church. People who attended took envelopes and put cash into them. They would mark the envelope for the operation of the church or for Terri and me. We actually were able each month to pay our bills and had money to help others.

Things were really growing within the group. I believed there was a calling on my life. Many young people were coming to me for ministry. There were constant phone calls from people in the group, asking me for help. I was giving out counsel, tainted by the harshness of our group's philosophy, but a lot of young people were coming to Jesus.

We believed we had the Word of God, and we were the ones who had the truth. We were young and uneducated, but we thought that made us purer and superior to leaders of other churches who actually attended seminaries or Bible schools. Looking back, I wonder how I could have given good counsel when I needed spiritual and emotional healing myself.

During this time, some of us were getting concerned what some people from the outside were thinking. Some of our members were actually getting kidnapped by their parents and sent to Christian deprogramming. This began around March of 1982. Some of the parents and members that had left believed that our group was now exhibiting cult-like tendencies. David, another elder, and I began to question Robert's leadership, wondering if we were going the wrong way. As we became more legalistic, community church leaders were speaking with us about their concerns privately, and we began to listen because Robert was not there to exert his influence.

I began to read the Book of Galatians. For a moment, the Lord was trying to speak to me about legalism and coming under a false covering of man. I told David and the other elder about the verses, and they tended to agree with me that we had become legalistic and that we needed to go to Spokane to correct Robert.

In the fall of 1982, we went to Spokane to confront Robert. At that time, there was also another older man with Robert who was from Ireland. He was the leader of another fellowship group that had started in Fernie, Canada. All of us had the same mindset. We all respected the leader from Ireland because he gave his home and belongings away while living in England to share the gospel message in Fernie. We thought of him as a Christian to look up to. Though he had some good qualities, he also had a harsh spirit and false doctrine and a false understanding about submission.

When we met with Robert, the Irish leader was with him as we began to share our concerns of legalism and harshness. Both of them began to tell us that we were self-righteous and in error. Robert went on about how all of us were acting like betrayers and Judases, and all of those who wanted unity with us were deceivers and Pharisees. We had nothing to say in response. They told me that they felt that the Lord wanted me to be the elder in charge of the group in Spokane. They explained I would move out to Spokane for a time with Robert, and then he would eventually return to Urbana. I allowed myself to be manipulated.

Somehow, I came away from this confrontation believing that Robert was the one who was right, and those who questioned him were off base. In Robert's mind, he knew the truth, and anyone who tried to tell him anything different had to be wrong. He was a prophet like Moses. Sadly, I was one of his yes-men, who encouraged his belief in his own infallibility.

Under the influence of an authoritative leader, I was like someone in a drunken stupor. Any question I had about faith or God was filtered through that influence. In my mind, Robert was getting truth from God that we needed to hear. Unfortunately, he replaced Jesus. Whenever we prayed to God to ask for wisdom, that wisdom had to line up with the answers Robert had for us.

When you accept someone else as a spiritual authority figure over you, you give up your will in deference to his will. In your own mind, you have given up your will to serve God. Of course, God really has nothing to do with it. I don't believe Robert was smart enough to take over a group, which began as a group of sincere young believers and transform it into a cult with him as its head. Satan knows how to use religion and charismatic people to destroy others. He works through people's ignorance and pride. Robert, me, and the other leaders had a big root of pride. It was a sin that we and others would pay for dearly.

There had to be something in Robert's and my heart, something in there that told us we wanted to be important, that we wanted to be somebody. This is not wrong in itself if you are of

Satan uses pride, religion, and false understanding of the Bible to lead people into cults which seem to be the only way to God, but are really just clever counterfeits.

a gentle and humble spirit and live for the benefit of others. But we were self-serving and not properly accountable to the word of God and other mature Christian leaders outside our group. My faith and that of others was interfered with. We feared and obeyed a man not God.

It became more important to me to be recognized as a leader in the group than to listen to the warnings that the group itself was corrupt. We needed a reformation like the church of old. This can come through one individual at a time, but sometimes the structure becomes so corrupt that it perpetuates this falsehood and the structure actually needs to be removed so the people can begin again from simple Christian beginnings.

I realize I made a conscious decision to stay with the group because it was appealing to me to have that leadership role which I would not have had anywhere else at such an early age. I preached to the congregation in Spokane and the church out there really liked me. I felt I had really connected with the people. Robert asked me to co-pastor the Spokane group with him for a short time as he prepared to return to Champaign-Urbana, Illinois.

Accepting this position was a very big mistake. It is one thing to say we were deceived and another to face the fact that this deception was unmasked countless times by people who left the group and additional Christian leaders who warned us. My pride got in the way of those warnings. I should have seriously considered running in the other direction. I got so caught up with the idea of being the leader of my own group that I ignored what was wrong with the group, its leaders, and its teachings. This was an additional bad decision and turning point for me.

By accepting this position, I was reaffirming Robert's leadership and authority as well. He was more than my report structure. Just like people who stay in any kind of sinful condition, there has to be cooperation between the sinner and the condition. I could have left at any time.

I moved out to Spokane with Terri, Melissa, and our son, Joseph, born a few months before on April 26, 1983. We lived in a nice duplex house. It was a beautiful city with mountains in the distance. We had church meetings in rented space not far from our home. At the time of my arrival, we had about eighty to 100 members. Right before my moving to Spokane, there were a few people kidnapped from the Spokane church by their parents and deprogrammed. My friend Jeff Goldberg was kidnapped and spent time with his family and deprogrammers. There were others kidnapped by their parents in Illinois as well. This should have been a warning sign for me to take a step back and examine why this was happening. Those who were kidnapped did not abandon their faith in Jesus. They just did not come back to the Fellowship.

Robert and his family moved back to Champaign-Urbana, Illinois in the spring of 1984. I was now the elder in charge.

Pride goes before destruction, a haughty spirit before a fall.
(Proverbs 16:18)

Chapter 10:

The Beginning of the End

On November 3, 1985, a key event occurred in the group in Champaign-Urbana. Robert Cline and others of his followers went into a church called Crusaders Church. They did an Old Testament prophet-like demonstration by throwing a cake into the church on the day of a church meeting, disrupting their meeting, and pronouncing judgment. The pastor of the Crusaders Church, Richard Jones, pressed criminal charges.

The *News-Gazette* reported the incident:

> "They prophesied in our church that our building would
> be destroyed. We see this as an issue of misguided individ-
> uals," Jones said. "We've got a situation here where there
> is a threat to lives and property."
>
> According to local ministers in Champaign-Urbana,
> it was about the time Cline returned to Urbana from
> Spokane that these types of demonstrations also took
> place at Urbana Assembly of God and New Covenant

Church. These men disrupted their services, hollering curses and chastising their worshipers.

As a result of the escalation, Pastor Jones pressed charges calling it mob action. The charge was a felony, carrying a penalty of probation to three years in prison and a fine of up to $10,000. They were also charged with criminal damage to property. After the trial in Urbana, Illinois, 11-day sentences in the county jail were given and a stiff fine."

I was not in Urbana when these demonstrations occurred, but I did fly in for the trial. At the time, I was totally deceived into thinking that we were doing the Lord's will. These types of disruptions also took place at a local Assembly of God through a new Fellowship group started by Robert Cline in Nutley, New Jersey. A new Fellowship group in Dallas, Texas, also carried out disruptions like this.

My church and I participated in three of these types of disruptions in Spokane, culminating at the New Covenant Church where James Leuschen was pastor at the time. I led a group of individuals with a clay pot filled with dirt and a huge boulder. We prophesied judgment from God and smashed the pot with the boulder. I was out of control. All the groups now had become people who had been deceived by false doctrine, and had given their wills over to follow a man, including me. I had allowed myself to become a puppet to Robert. I and others were emulating our leader, but the reality was that we had allowed this to happen to ourselves.

From Bad to Worse

There was no contrition concerning the trial in Urbana, so the wrong direction only got worse. Harsh discipline escalated to members' wives and children in all the fellowships. Wives more and more felt that they were losing their ability to give their husbands their opinion if something appeared wrong to them. Men and women who questioned the leaders were also losing their ability to speak their concerns. Adults were actually spanked in the groups in Champaign, Dallas, Clifton, and Spokane.

In 1987, Robert Cline made a trip to Spokane where I was the elder in charge. A ten-year-old boy named, Alan Peters, came forward with his parents in a service to receive prayer from the leaders. This young boy had symptoms of a serious illness. He was eating constantly, urinating very often, and he did not feel well. Instead of addressing the medical symptoms, Robert began questioning the boy and his parents about his personal life. His parents said the boy was masturbating with his friends. Robert said he was an evil little boy and that God was judging him. This is why he was sick and he would have to repent.

After the service, we went to the boy's home with his parents. Robert told them that he thought that his sickness was a result of his sin. I remember Robert quoting to me Bible verses about young evil kings in the Hebrew Scriptures. He compared Alan to one of these kings.

A man named John, who belonged to the congregation, was a diabetic. He told us he believed Alan's symptoms indicated he had diabetes.

My wife Terri looked up the symptoms in a medical manual and said, "Jeff, I think he has diabetes. He needs to go to the doctor."

I should have listened to my wife, but instead I listened to Robert. I had been preaching that the Lord could heal, and there was a lot of pressure coming out of the preaching not to see a doctor. This was almost like the Christian Science doctrine. I was the pastor in Spokane, so I was responsible for this preaching

While we were praying for the boy, he was getting sicker and sicker. His father, George Peters, called our home one night and told Robert that he was greatly concerned for Alan. He was really sick and he was concerned that the boy could die. Robert and his wife were staying at our home at the time and he came to our room to answer George's phone call.

Terri and I heard Robert say to Alan's father, "Your son is going to live. He's not going to die."

It was a terrible scene. Robert so wanted to see Alan healed by the Lord that he told this to George. George, wanting to prove his faith to Robert, me, and all the leaders, did not call an ambulance. When Janice, the boy's mother, expressed her concern to her husband about the boy's health, with Robert's encouragement, George proceeded to spank his wife.

Shortly after that, we received a phone call at home, George Peters, the boy's father, saw Alan wasn't breathing. It was early Sunday morning and we were getting ready for church when we received the call. All the leaders went to the Peters' home, about six or seven of us. Alan had died. Although it might seem obvious now that this would happen, we were so deceived that we did not see it coming.

We had presumed on God, believing that He was going to heal this child if *we* had the faith. This was a doctrine of condemnation. If someone doubted, they would tend to feel condemned and try to prove their faith. If healing did not come, the questions came, "What is wrong with me? Am I sinning? Am I in the sin of unbelief?" We all came under this false understanding of faith.

The death of Alan Peters occurred December 20, 1987. The boy was lying lifeless on his parents' bed. The Peters called a funeral home, the funeral home called the coroner, who called the police. When that boy died, something within me died. I was a completely broken man. Up to that point I had believed that the teaching I heard from Robert was true. It took the death of this boy for me to wake up and realize that the abuse and false doctrine was a big lie.

An investigation took place. There was an autopsy. The conclusion was that Alan died because of untreated diabetes. This was considered gross negligence.

It was explained to us that there was going to be an investigation into the negligence. Robert and other leaders proceeded to remove me from my job as pastor and kick me out of the Fellowship. I realized as time went by that Robert needed a scapegoat to attempt to get out of trouble. People were really mad at me because of what I had taught and had lived. Now, I was the one who had to leave the church. I had reaped what I had sown. The years of wrong I had done were now coming back to haunt me. People in the group were remorseful about what had happened, but they were still loyal for a while to Robert. The deception was beginning to be revealed for what it was, but they were confused at the time.

Each person had to face God on their own and come to grips with what had happened.

My Life Was Totally Shattered

We had progressed from being a fellowship filled with zealous young people who thought they were following the Lord to realizing that we were following a man and had become a full-fledged cult. We had fallen into legalism, abuse, and the extreme idea of excluding medicine and doctors. Now a child had died.

It would take a period of time for people to find good churches and true Christian ministry to bring healing to all the abuse that took place in this group.

My wife and I packed hastily to move back to Champaign-Urbana. We had just had our third child, Benjamin, on July 2, 1987. He was just a baby. I had a wife and three children to support, but I had no job and no prospects in sight. I had shamed the name of the Lord. I had let my wife, family, and friends down. My life was totally shattered.

I met with the group in Champaign-Urbana, but that became an ugly scene. People stood up and called out their complaints against me, telling me what I had done to them in the past. I was already crushed because of the boy's death in Spokane, and now I was pelted with additional complaints from people who I thought were my friends. There was a spirit of harshness and vengeance in the meeting room, and it all seemed directed at me. I was getting back what I had put into the fellowship.

No matter what I said in apology to them, people kept saying, "You're not repentant."

I was in shock. A human being had died. I felt like I had been struck by lightning. Apparently they wanted to see me break down and cry, as if that would prove that I was truly repentant. I was beyond crying or even feeling anything. It was as if I were not really there anymore; I was just an empty shell.

The Fellowship groups throughout the country totally collapsed after this incident.

I went to Terri and said, "I shamed you. I've hurt you. I've hurt many others. Why don't you leave me? I feel like I have committed the unpardonable sin. If you divorce me, you can find someone else and make a good life for yourself."

From her point of view, our marriage had not ended. In fact, it had just begun. While she was not thrilled with the idea of having me in prison for my bad decisions, she was happy this horrible group had collapsed.

Terri replied, "I finally have back the guy I married. I committed my life to you, and I will keep that commitment. I feel that now we have a better chance of making it because there is no way we will ever let anybody else have power over us, or to tell us what we should do or not do."

We had very few possessions at that time. We lived in a small, rented apartment. We had a Toyota Corolla and Toyota minivan. I needed to sell the minivan to retain a lawyer to walk me through the charges that were coming in Spokane. I had to get cash quickly, so I sold it for about two thirds of what it was worth.

As the buyer drove away with our family van, I saw my whole life going up in smoke. I felt close to a nervous breakdown. I was holding my infant son, Benjamin, and he felt like he weighed 1,000 pounds. I went into the bathroom and hung my head over the sink and cried out to the Lord.

"I am so sorry for what I have done, and for the lie that I have lived. I feel like my life is over. Please forgive me."

I felt like I was on the verge of a total meltdown. When I finished that prayer, Terri said there was a phone call for me. It was Toby Kahr. About a week before this, I had gone to the University of Illinois to the Office of Human Resources. I asked to see Toby Kahr. I was told that he moved to Chapel Hill, North Carolina. Someone gave me his address, and I went home and wrote him a letter. It was a cry for help. I could barely lift the pen as I wrote him. To this day I don't even remember what I wrote to him.

Now Toby was calling me, "I have heard about all the things that have happened in Spokane. My son, you are going to be okay. Rita and I want to help you. I have prayed for eight years that God would break this deception and set you free of it. I have believed for all these years that God would fully redeem you."

Then Toby and Rita invited our whole family to come to Chapel Hill for a visit, "Would you come stay in our home for a little bit? Perhaps God will help you to start over with a brand new life."

A Glimmer of Hope

Within days, we decided to go visit. I believed that I had committed the unpardonable sin, that I was the most evil man on the face of the earth. But as we were driving to North Carolina, I felt a glimmer of hope.

Toby and Rita began ministering to Terri and me, trying to help lift me out of the abyss of despair. They shared with me that repentance was not about feelings. It's not about how much you cry. To repent is to have a sincere, contrite heart before the Lord, and to make a decision to change direction.

I looked back at what had taken place in our group. So many things we did were so artificial. People would cry in open meetings, saying they were repentant

"After you face God, you might cry, but the Lord is looking for a simple change of heart," Toby and Rita said.

for various sins. But they were really just afraid, terrified of being abused, humiliated, or expelled. Can anybody really change under such conditions?

Not only did I go in the entirely wrong direction, but I actually thought that I had been following the Lord in doing it. I let my family and friends down. I even let the Lord down. I was thinking to myself, *Should I just end it all by taking my life and make things easier for Terri and the children and those I have hurt?*

I remembered a story in the Bible about a man named Judas. He was one of the original twelve apostles that walked with Jesus. He was the treasurer and kept the money for them. This man was a thief, and took money out of the treasury for himself. In the end he betrayed the Lord for thirty pieces of silver. This man would have done anything for a buck. When he later came to himself after the crucifixion of Jesus, he felt remorse and gave the money back to the chief priests and elders. Then he committed suicide.

Many thieves and betrayers who have repented of their sins are now some the most trusted of Christians and human beings and live productive lives in their communities. We are spirit beings. Our real person is encased in this body of flesh. When we die, we must account for our life before God. We continue to live on in eternity, living in Heaven with God or separated from Him in Hell. God has given all authority and judgment to His Son, Jesus. He is the judge. Life does not end; it is on an eternal time clock which means we live forever.

God does not put people in Hell. We choose Hell by saying to God, "Jesus' sacrifice was not enough for our sin. I am, too, bad."

God wants us in Heaven and that is why He came Himself in the form of human flesh as our Savior.

I realized that committing suicide would only make things worse and slap God in the face by saying that the blood He shed on the cross was not thick enough to atone for my sins committed against mankind and Him. As I prayed outside of the influences of the Fellowship, the Lord made it very clear to me that I would be disciplined by Him for my wrongdoing. He also made it clear to me that He is the judge. I do not have the right to have a judgmental attitude towards others or even myself. I just needed to agree with Him that my actions were wrong and He is right.

Repentance means to have a change of heart and to change my actions. I also realized that I must do all I could to make amends with those I had hurt. I realized even if my situation seemed hopeless, I needed to get right with God and see what He would want me to do. It was His plan for my life and I needed to give Him the opportunity to take a bad situation and do something good with it.

Toby and Rita Kahr, Pastor Paul Gordon of Christian Assembly Church in Durham, N.C., and others said that the Lord wanted to give me a brand new beginning. I began reading the Bible, and in Romans 2:4 it says that God is longsuffering and the goodness of God leads to repentance. God may allow us to reap what we sow in a good or bad sense. But even when we do, if we fully got what we fully deserved, we would never be able to stand it. God is much more patient and forbearing than I ever could be. His character is such that He does not want to leave any of us behind. He just asks that we have a change of heart and learn from our mistakes. Some mistakes have huge consequences. With the help of Toby and Rita, I began to see God as He really is, a God of mercy and compassion.

Could God really take a broken life, put it back together, and bring hope and fulfillment?

Or do you show contempt for the riches of his kindness, tolerance and patience, not realizing that God's kindness leads you toward repentance?
(Romans 2:4)

Chapter 11:

Batter Up or Facing Up

They called me from Spokane and told what the charges were against me, and that I had to attend an arraignment hearing. Robert Cline was to be arraigned at the same time as me, and I did not look forward to seeing him.

Attorney Rick Bechtolt accompanied us to the courtroom where we were to be arraigned. He was the one Robert had hired to represent him, and who let Robert and me know that we had to return to Spokane for this hearing.

The *News-Gazette*, AP reported: "The arraignment was April 21, 1988, for second degree criminal mistreatment, a class C felony. George and Janice Peters were charged with homicide by abuse, a Class A felony, with a penalty of up to thirty years in prison. Criminal mistreatment charges were also filed against a Fellowship leader from the Urbana Fellowship, and two other leaders from Spokane. The *News-Gazette* reported: "The statements made to the sheriff showed that the group believed illness is caused by sin and a lack of faith in God."

The judge read the charges to me. He said they could carry up to five years in prison, told me what my bail was, and that I was going to need a lawyer. I knew that so I had already sold the van. I was fingerprinted at the county jail, but I did not have the entire $20,000 bond. My parents helped me post ten percent of the bail, while the bondsman posted the rest. Later, after I appeared in court, the bondsman kept the ten percent that I posted.

Four of us were charged in the death of the boy—his mother and father, Robert Cline, and I. The other leaders who had been involved in the group had been let off the hook in exchange for providing information on the group.

Looking in the *Yellow Pages*, I found a lawyer named, Alan Gauper. He told me he would talk with the prosecutor and find out what he was planning to do.

It was all a frightening process, but later I saw it as the way God used to correct my life.

The lawyer seemed sympathetic concerning the felony charge. He said he did not believe I was guilty according to the letter of the law. He asked if I held a gun to these people's heads, telling them they could not see a doctor. He said that ultimately it was the parents' responsibility to get their child to the doctor. There was an additional charge against me for participating in the spanking of a young woman. This was a misdemeanor charge that carried up to a year in jail.

Both charges carried a total of six years in jail, but he did not give me any false hope either. He had photographs of the boy at the time of his death. He said this could inflame the jury, causing them to go by their emotions instead of the letter of the law.

"What really makes this bad," the lawyer said, "is that it is one thing for a child to die from a lack of medical attention, but another to spank a child who is dying."

While I had not been directly involved with spanking the boy, the lawyer said I would be viewed as part of that incident.

"If the prosecutor wants to take this case to the limit," said my lawyer, a former prosecutor himself, "he will use every trick he can to inflame the jury. The jury can be swept along in a wave of emotion."

Afraid, I realized I could go to prison for a long time.

I was facing an uncertain future, but at least I had a lawyer, some good friends, and God on my side.

Although the judge had ordered us not to talk to each other, Robert contacted me. He said that the parents were responsible to take their child to the doctor. Although this was true, we all were wrong in the death of this child. This concerned me, and my eyes continued to open. In my mind, Robert had orchestrated the whole direction of the four days when Alan died. It is not that I believed I was innocent; I could have called 911. But the idea that the one supreme leader of the entire cult would make one last attempt to save his own skin at the expense of the mother of the child was absolutely disappointing to me. I realized exactly what kind of person I had been following. In the end, he really didn't care about anyone but himself. He would say he cared, but from my perspective it was all a lie, at least at this time in his life.

Being away from the group and receiving Christian counseling in Chapel Hill caused me to see clearly the way I treated people, the false doctrine I taught, and how I came under a false spiritual covering. I wanted to make a clean break from Robert and all false religion.

I realized that I should never follow a man. By doing so, I opened myself up to every evil thing that followed.

I also realized that the mom, Janice Peters, was totally innocent as she was trying to tell George and Robert that she was uncomfortable with the whole situation. I felt bad for Janice; she did not participate in anything wrong; she just wanted her son to live.

Before I returned home from Spokane, I went to New Covenant where I had done my prophetic demonstration and asked Pastor Jim Leuschen for forgiveness from him and his church. He was so kind and told me that his church was praying for my deliverance from the deception I had lived under. They offered me the right hand of fellowship and I was so grateful for his friendship.

Jim was very instrumental in encouraging me that the Lord, as well as he and his church, had forgiven me for my sin. He encouraged me to forgive myself, and that if I would walk faithful now and in the future, the Lord would use it all for good. He and his wife, Marsha, are beautiful, kind examples of Christian forgiveness and reconciliation. He, his wife, and their church represented many other examples of the hope that waited as time unfolded.

While waiting for a trial date, I returned to Chapel Hill to resume my life with my family. We lived with Toby and Rita for about four months. Then, through friends of theirs and ours, Reid and Katie Shaffer, I landed a job with General Electric at Research Triangle Park near Durham. It was a pretty good job, testing computer chips. I was making a decent wage, but there were no benefits. We were able to move out of Toby's house into our own small, two-bedroom apartment. We had three children and lived in a modest complex behind the projects in Chapel Hill.

We received tremendous support from Toby and Rita Kahr and the people at Christian Assembly Church in Durham. Pastor Paul Gordon was a Jewish believer and the people in the congregation were some of the most gracious and kind people one could ever meet. They knew everything about me, but what I had done did not seem to matter to them. They explained to me that the Lord knew I was repentant and wanted to heal my family and me. Pastor Paul Gordon was a kind man who just wanted to help us have a new life in Jesus Christ.

I knew that God saved people for eternity, but I had big questions: *Is He able to save me now? Can I get right with the Lord?* Toby, Rita, Paul, and the whole Christian Assembly Church assured me that the Lord had forgiven me, but there would be consequences for my sin and that would be up to the Lord. It was beyond my comprehension that the Lord could forgive the terrible deeds that I had committed, but I chose to believe by faith. I also realized that I was going to suffer the consequences of my bad decisions.

Like a father who loves his children, God sometimes allows the consequences of our bad decisions to correct us so that we decide not to make certain choices ever again.

I would have to accept whatever correction the Lord had for me with a humble heart. It seems to me, in a sense, I was saved twice. We may only be saved once in the biblical and eternal sense, but I believe God saves us in many ways over and over again. When I initially read the Bible and saw Jesus as Savior and God, repented for my sins and believed by faith, I was saved. When I allowed somebody to interfere with my biblical understanding, the Lord came to my rescue and corrected me, making it clear that I was to read the Bible for myself, draw my own conclusions, and never allow anyone to manipulate me again.

The Trial

The trial date was set in October of 1988. I decided to return to Spokane with Terri and Benjamin a few weeks early. Toby and Rita were watching our two older children. Terri and I stayed with friends from New Covenant Fellowship. During the time in their home, I asked myself, *why am I going to trial? What is there to defend? How could I defend my innocence when I knew I was guilty?* I figured that going to trial would only make the judge mad.

I said to Terri, "I'm not innocent."

She said, "I knew that all along. You had a responsibility to get that boy to the doctor. You were a contributing factor in Alan's death."

"I agree," I said. "I was wrong. I need to go with my lawyer and see the prosecuting attorney, be honest, and plead guilty. Maybe he will be merciful if he knows that I realize my wrong doing."

Terri agreed with me that this was the right thing to do. We agreed that I needed to make this right with the Lord and man. No matter the price, I would have to pay. I was also concerned for the mom, Janice Peters. I hoped that the prosecutor would let her go if he knew that she was dominated and could not get her child to the doctor. She tried to stop the boy from being spanked by Robert and the father the day before his death. She had no control over his receiving medical care, because her husband forbade it. As a result of my testimony to the prosecutor, the charges were dropped against the boy's mother before her trial was to begin.

I was facing a ninety-day sentence for criminal mistreatment, according to the standard sentencing guidelines in the death of the boy, and an additional year for assault in the spanking of the young woman. I decided to plead guilty to the charges against me because I believed I was guilty. My lawyer entered a plea of guilty for me on Wednesday, October 5, 1988, for the charges of felony second-degree criminal mistreatment and misdemeanor assault.

"About a week later, Robert Cline also pled guilty to second-degree criminal mistreatment. Cline admitted that he spanked the boy three or four times to put an end to the boy's defiance" (*News-Gazette*).

I met with my lawyer, who set up a meeting with the prosecuting attorney about five days before the trial. I told him the truth about what had happened within the group. The prosecutor said he didn't want to see me go to prison. He thought justice would be served better if I were to speak in public about the dangers of cults, to warn others not to get involved with them. We met with the assistant state's attorney in his office.

He said, "This is the hardest case for me to try. It is hard for me to sleep at night, especially because it involves Christian people. I believe these were good people who got caught up in a bad situation. I would prefer if you did not go to prison. I don't believe sending you to prison will serve the state. But regardless of my recommendation, the judge has the discretion to give you any sentence of his choosing."

The judge could take any recommendations into consideration, but would ultimately determine whatever sentence he deemed appropriate.

Meanwhile, I had agreed to testify as a prosecution witness in the case of the boy's father. He was charged with first-degree manslaughter. On October 17, 1988, I testified that George Peters was free to take his son to the hospital, even though our cult preached against conventional medicine. In court, I recalled what George Peters had said when he and the elders discussed taking his son to the hospital the day before his death: "My heart is in faith, and I don't want to do that at this point in time" (*News-Gazette*). My testimony was not intended to hurt George Peters, or help him, just to tell the truth as I understood it. I had told the truth to the prosecutor regarding my own involvement, and I felt compelled to also tell the truth regarding the father.

In a packed courtroom, I explained to the judge how many had left the Fellowship, and that of those who were there to the end, all were under the influence of deception.

"Looking back, having to do things over again, everything would have been totally different," I said. George Peters' defense was that the church leaders had so much control over him that he could not have obtained medical help for his son. Mr. Peters was found guilty of first-degree manslaughter and sentenced to forty-one months.

The judge in the case said to Mr. Peters, "You are ultimately responsible for your son's care."

The judge sentenced Robert Cline to thirty-six months in prison. On November 14, 1988, I went before the judge and the prosecutor made his recommendation of ninety days. The judge did not agree with him.

He said, "Why is it that it takes a tragedy to realize that what they have been doing is wrong? Medicine has been given to us by God as much as the power of prayer."

He was right. He also said that he had an obligation to send a message to anyone who might be interested in starting a religious cult.

I was sentenced to twenty-four months for the charge of criminal mistreatment and six months concurrent for the spanking of a member of the Fellowship. He told me that I would be eligible to go home after sixteen months and begin a new life. The judge told me to go home for about three months, get my personal affairs in order, and then report mid-February to begin my sentence.

Terri was shocked and cried with the length of time involved; Toby, Rita, and Paul Gordon were upset as well. In the end, I believed that the Lord had the judge's heart in his hand and knew what was best for me and all concerned. I believe that the Lord wanted to demonstrate His justice for all, and that when I got out of prison, no one could say that I did not pay a price for my wrong doing. He is a brilliant Father. My negligent decisions caused me to be where I was. How could I actually atone for the death of a human being? My sentence was actually God's mercy to me. In my heart I was not surprised. The Lord was right and I was wrong!

When Terri and I returned home, with the weight of the shame I felt in my heart, I again asked her and the children to forgive me. Melissa was about seven years old and Joseph about five. Benjamin, at one year old, was too young to know what was going on.

Again I said to Terri, "I am not deserving of you, consider leaving me."

She said, "I will not leave you and I will be waiting when you get home. Don't bring this up again. I finally have back the man I originally married. When you get home, the Lord will provide us with a new life. We will have each other and our children, and with the Lord's help, we will rebuild our lives."

The real hero of this story is my wife, Terri. She was a true Christian testimony of God's love and heart for me when I was not deserving of any good thing. I witnessed the true unconditional love of God when I turned from my sin. He put His heart in Terri to forgive and never forsake me. God had a plan beyond my understanding, and now I had to take one day at a time.

> *"For I know the plans I have for you," declares the Lord,*
> *"Plans to prosper you and not to harm you,*
> *plans to give you hope and a future."*
> (Jeremiah 29:11 NIV)

Chapter 12:

Prison Time

When the time came for me to leave Chapel Hill to go to prison, the congregation at Christian Assembly prayed over me. When they prayed over me, there was not a dry eye in the room.

Pastor Paul Gordon said, "You are going to prison a repentant man. We believe in you and believe in your future. We are going to support your family while you are gone."

It was really difficult to see Toby Kahr crying over me. Despite the uplifting words and numerous prayers, this was the lowest point of my life.

My wife and three children lived in the apartment near the housing projects. How could Terri go to work? She had three young children to take care of, including a one-year-old baby. I was deeply unsettled in my heart about leaving my family in these circumstances. I had to learn to trust in God to take care of all of us.

The church was faithful in helping. They sent $150 to my wife every month while I was incarcerated. Toby also helped out, sending $150 each month. Terri's parents sent $300 each month. My brother, Rick, helped as well as my mom. Our rent was $325 a month. God provided exactly what Terri needed. She cleaned houses to add to the family income.

During this time period Terri attended a routine, parent-teacher conference with our son's kindergarten teacher. The conference was positive with the teacher sharing with Terri about Joe's progress and what a smart boy he was. At the end of the meeting the teacher ask Terri if everything was alright at home because when Joe drew pictures in class, all the people in his pictures were crying. Terri was stunned and saddened by her comment because she had done her best to shield the children from the situation and provide them with a positive, nurturing environment. Terri told the teacher the truth—that his father was in prison. The teacher was very kind and told Terri to please let her know if there was anything she could do to help.

My bad decisions had dragged me to the point where not only was I going to be incarcerated, but my wife and children were going to have to make it without me for a while. It was hard for me to think about what they were going through, what it meant for them to have a husband and a dad in prison 3,000 miles away. Maybe it was better to be that far away, so they would never have to see me in prison.

I took a plane to Spokane to report to prison. On February 14, 1989, I reported to the county jail in Spokane. I gave up my clothes and all personal belongings and was given inmate clothes. I was put in a cell all by myself. The door of my cell slammed shut! I was an absolutely broken man. This was my first evening of a sixteen-month dark-night journey.

The next day, the deputies in charge handcuffed and chained me to other inmates. They put me on a bus to go to the Shelton Receiving Center in a different part of the state. It was the ultimate humiliation of my life!

I was placed in a receiving and holding prison for about six weeks while the authorities decided what to do with me. In my first days in prison, I saw a transvestite eating in the dining hall during our meals. In my state of ignorance, I was amazed to see "her" eating with us. I actually thought we had a woman inmate.

"What is a woman doing in here?" I asked one of the inmates.

"That isn't a woman," the inmates said, laughing. "That's a man."

I was shaken by this. As I went back to my cell I thought of things I had heard, about sexual perversions taking place within prisons. I thought, if this guy comes near me, he will regret it. In my cell, I cried out to the Lord.

The Lord said to me, "What do you see around you?"

I said, "I see the lights are on in my cell."

"But you are in the midst of great spiritual darkness," the Lord said to me.

Then the Lord began dealing with me concerning the transvestite, "Whose sin is worse, this man's or yours?"

"Mine is, because I should have known better," I said. "I came to know You and fell into deception."

"That is correct," the Lord said to me. "But I broke the deception in your life and brought light into your darkness instead. I gave you understanding of what was wrong. This man has been deceived also. I am able to open his eyes as well. That is why Jesus died. Jesus died for the sins of all people, so they could be set free. When you repented of your sins, I forgave you. Do not have a harsh attitude toward this man or anyone else in this prison."

The Lord began teaching me about physical prisons and spiritual prisons. Spiritual prisons can actually be worse. Some people are in prison for not doing any crimes, like Paul in the Bible. He was put in prison over and over again for his faith. He was free in prison to share his faith in Christ. People are bound in terrible sin and are spiritually imprisoned by drugs, alcohol, sex, pornography, lying, eating, etc. My spiritual prison led to this physical prison. The Lord had set me free of my spiritual deception, now I had to physically pay my debt to society.

At times during the night in this place, I could hear many of the men screaming and making loud noises when I tried to go to sleep. I hated the loud noises and wished it would stop. This was a very dark place! Weeping and gnashing of teeth!

From Shelton Receiving Center, I was sent to a logging camp near Seattle, on the other side of the state. This was not a hardcore prison. This was a minimum-security prison. Every day we went out into the forest to cut down trees. We learned how to cut down hardwood trees in the forests. The purpose was to thin newly planted forests so that the other trees could grow big and tall.

The Department of Natural Resources taught us how to use a chain saw and maintain it. We had a crew of multiple people cutting down trees in different areas. The trees were not that tall so it only took one person per tree to cut it down. After we cut a tree down, we would saw it in many pieces for it to decay and break down in the forest. We also had the opportunity to plant new trees in areas where trees had been cut down.

One night in our barracks, a young man named Anthony came over to my bed as I was getting ready to go to sleep. He was about twenty-five years old, five-foot-four-inches tall, dark complexion, and black curly hair.

He said, "Jeff, I know that you're a Christian. I'm full of demons, and I want to kill somebody. I am so angry. I want you to pray for me and deliver the demons out of me."

At that time, I did not want to tell anyone I was a Christian. I felt that I had been a hypocrite. I had been cast into prison, where I deserved to be, and I didn't want to have the Lord's name on my lips ever again. I shamed His name.

In my mind, I prayed, "God, here is someone who desperately needs ministry. But I shamed Your name, and I am the last one on earth who should be working for You. I am in prison here, without any ability to help anyone."

Anthony persisted, shaking me, and asking for deliverance from his demons. Reluctantly, I got out of bed, went to the duty station, and spoke with the officer in charge. It turned out that this man was a Christian. I told him what Anthony wanted me to do.

His response surprised me, "You have my permission to take him out on the rear dock and pray for him," the officer said. "Just don't let him run away. In a few minutes, I will join you out there as well."

I waited for the officer to join us, and then we both put our hands on Anthony and prayed, "Lord, I don't know what to pray. I don't know how to deliver anybody. But You do. In the name of Jesus, I command these demons to come out of this man."

We heard sounds coming from Anthony, as if he was choking.

"Keep praying, the demons are coming out," Anthony said, as he fought for his breath.

I kept praying, "In the name of Jesus, come out of him."

Anthony shouted, "Keep going, and keep praying."

Then Anthony shouted, "They're out. They're out. I'm free, I'm free."

During the following days and weeks, Anthony would show up at my bed almost every night. Anthony told me about all the abuse he went through in his life. His father was on death row in Walla-Walla, Washington, a hard core penitentiary. When he was a child, his mother's boyfriend would chain him to a wall in his basement and beat him. Anthony said he once ran to a pastor's house down the street for help, but neither he nor anybody else ever came to his rescue.

"Nobody cared," Anthony told me.

I didn't know what Anthony did to be imprisoned. I never asked him. The inmates rarely talked about what they did to land in prison, unless it was about the drugs they did or if they thought something they did made them famous in the eyes of other prisoners or their own. Yet, I felt like I was gaining insight into the background of prisoners. I was beginning to see what it was like to be a lost soul, someone who did not know God and was surrounded by darkness for most of his life. Because of my shame, I did not take time to lead him to the Lord. This Divine Encounter began to show me that the Lord was not done with me. It was also a time of learning.

To pass time, we played fast pitch softball with some black athletes, most of whom were in this prison for drug-related crimes. When we played softball, I was usually one of the best players, and they all wanted to get to know me. There was a homosexual, Mark who also had an interest in the Bible.

One day the inmates confronted me and said, "Siegel, we know why you are here. We actually planned out our crimes, but yours was not planned out."

I explained to them that I was no different than them as I deserved to be here, but I had made peace with God because I was sorry for what I had done.

I would find groups of inmates, big black studs, Hispanics, white athletic kind of guys, and this little homosexual druggy, all hanging out and asking me about the Bible. I began to realize that I was in the midst of lost souls—lost to the ravages of sin. This is who Jesus died for, those who needed a physician, and those who needed spiritual healing.

Jesus is the only one who can fix a human being.

Those who are sick down deep usually know it. This is why these guys wanted to hang out with me. They knew they were empty inside. I shared as they questioned me, but was not ready to minister or lead anyone to Christ.

The Logging Crew

We went out every day, in the back of a van, which carried fifteen passengers or so, as part of a logging crew to work in the forests. We didn't have to wear prison uniforms. We just wore logger's clothes: blue jeans, work shirts, and blue jean jackets.

Some of the other crew members would smoke marijuana on the way out to our work sites. I would have to inhale the smoke, which I felt was dangerous for a number of reasons. Every so often the prison officials would give us urinalysis tests, called a UA. I believed that if I was given a UA and tested positive because of second-hand smoke they could ship me to a hard-core prison. I definitely did not want to go to a worse prison. I felt that this was a risk to my going home, but more importantly, I felt it was a risk to my survival.

One day, as we were working in the forest cutting trees, a tall Douglas Fir tree came crashing down near me, a little too close for comfort. I realized the culprit was Mark. He was proud of his sexual orientation and, although I didn't agree with it, I was kind to him. I did not appreciate his dropping a heavy Douglas Fir tree so close that it could have killed me if I had not been looking. Mark had been smoking pot on the way to the forest and in the forest as well. I was fed up and had had enough.

One of the things you are not supposed to do in prison is tell on your fellow inmates. I did not want to be killed by a pothead or shipped off to a real slammer for the rest of my time. At the same time, I did not relish the idea of inmates coming after me to exact retribution. I believed I was putting my life on the line if I reported the pot smokers.

I decided to trust in the Lord, for once in my life, in the midst of a very frightening situation. I realized that I had to begin to walk with the Lord in the midst of my correction from Him, and not wait until I got out. I went to the crew boss and told him about the pot smoking. By informing, I had just traded one set of risks for another. I was "snitching" on inmates, which is not the safest kind of activity to participate in when these are the guys you are living with. When the pot smokers realized that I was the snitch, they were very angry. One day they cornered me near our dorm. The leader of the pot smokers was in on an assault charge.

"We know the only one who could have told on us was you, Siegel," he growled.

It seemed that this man in particular must have been getting into trouble over and over again concerning this issue. He asked me if I was the one who told on him, and I held my peace. I could not lie, but my silence became my confession. I just walked away. A lot of the black athletic guys that I played softball with came to my aid saying that they would protect me, but I realized that I was in real trouble.

At the end of each workday, we would go into a TV room, kick back, and watch the tube. That night, as I was walking to the TV room, it was as if the Spirit of God was warning me, "Don't go in there. Go to your dorm room and to your bed immediately."

When I went to my bed, the officer who had prayed with me was there, and asked, "Siegel, are you in some kind of trouble?"

It was as if he knew what was going on. The word of this incident must have been spreading quickly.

I told him what had happened and he said, "Come with me."

I was placed into an area called, "The Hole," in solitary confinement for ten days for protective custody. The solitary confinement cells were for prisoners who could not get along with others, who were being punished for some infraction of the rules or violent act, or for protective custody. All I had in that cell was a Gideon Bible. At first it seemed like my life had just gone from bad to worse. These cells were in a confined area with bars but no windows. A toilet and a bed lined the wall.

Sensing God was there with me in a special way, I felt the awesome burden of my own sins like I had never felt it before. I held the Bible up above my head and cried out, "Dear God, you delivered Joseph from the pit his brothers had thrown him in, and you delivered him from prison, which he did not deserve. I am here in prison, which I deserve. I am not asking you to deliver me. I just want to tell you again that I am sorry for my sins."

God reached out to me and said, "I'm not done with you. You're still mine. I really want to save you. Will you come back to me? I will take you back; you are one of my children; and I do not reject you."

Then I had a vision of a man riding on a bicycle. He started going very fast. Suddenly, the wheels jammed and came to a sudden stop. That man flew over the handlebars and hurt himself very badly, skinned up and bleeding with open wounds. However, the bicycle was not damaged.

"You were the man riding the bicycle," the Lord said to me. "There was nothing wrong with the bicycle. There was something wrong with you. The bicycle was the Word of God. You were reading my Word under the influence of people telling you what the Bible said, or how to ride the bike. You don't need anyone to tell you what the Bible means. I have given you my Holy Spirit. As you read the Bible, allow the Spirit to show you what the words mean. He is your teacher, not men."

"You are going to have to get back on the bicycle. You are going to read the Bible again, under My influence, and not under man's influence. Do not let others get in the way of our relationship ever again. All I ever wanted was to have you to Myself. I am here for you always; just keep in contact each day. Spend time with Me and in time you will come to know

My love, mercy, and provision. The worst part of your life is over. From this day forward, I am going to turn your life around."

The next day the guard came to my cell with a letter from a man I had never met, John Oakley. John was a friend of Steve Bush. I had met Steve at The New Covenant Church in Spokane when I asked the church to forgive me. He told me the day I repented, that he saw me do it with all of my heart. He said that he'd never done anything with all his heart. He said that I had misdirected energy, and now my repentance was whole-hearted. He was under conviction that the Lord wanted all of his heart.

John had received a settlement for an eye injury in which he had received enough money to buy two Taco Bells and a Roadhouse Family Style Restaurant. Steve had asked John to help me out. Steve had no idea I was in solitary confinement at the time.

This letter was written to the Department of Corrections, but came addressed to me on the envelope. It was a miracle that it even got to me. It was a request to release me to John Oakley's home so I could work in one of his restaurants during work release the final five or six months of my time. I gave the prison guard the letter to pass on to my counselor. Ten days later, I was told that I was being sent across the state to Pine Lodge Minimum Security Prison. Then I would go to Pre-Release and on to live in a halfway house in a work release program.

Because I now lived in North Carolina, it had earlier been determined that I was ineligible for work release because I had no place in Washington to which I could be released. I no longer lived there. But John Oakley's request was honored, making his home my home of release point. This was a Christian man whom I had never even met. Is this a miracle or what? The Lord was lightening my load when I did not deserve it.

Even though I was hundreds of miles away from the prison near the logging camp, the word somehow followed me to Spokane that I had snitched. There is something called a "snitch jacket" that is put on you in prison situations if you have told on someone. Death threats were left on my bed at Pine Lodge. These threats had me concerned. Many of the inmates had drugs hidden and were afraid of me.

One of the inmates came to speak with me at lunch in the dining hall. He had Indian blood in his family background and he played on the prison softball team. He came over to my table, said he knew what had happened in the logger's camp, and began to threaten me.

I called Toby Kahr on the phone and told him of my circumstances, and he said, "Either God is who He said He is, or He's not. He will protect you and you must put all your trust in Him. Put your hand in His each day and watch what He will do."

The snitch jacket, a terrible black cloud on an inmate's reputation, was lifted off me through an unusual set of circumstances. One day the prison held the Inmate Olympics. One of the events was the ball throw, with a baseball on a baseball diamond. Everyone took a turn throwing the baseball from home plate towards the left field fence. The biggest and strongest looking guys threw their balls, which landed, in the outfield. I went last. I reared back and let the ball fly, aiming to throw the ball over the outfield fence. The ball sailed, not quite out of the park, but came very close to the outfield fence, about fifty feet farther than anyone else's throw. My competitors, who considered themselves the biggest, baddest, most macho studs in the history of the world, stood there stunned. These Goliaths of the Northwest had been hit between the eyes by a dirty little snitch from the flatlands.

I tried to fill the time with positive things like taking different courses, learning to type and use computers, anything to make the time go by faster. In my spare time, I would go to the curio shop to work with clay. I would make things like lamps, piggy banks, anything to pass the time. One day a bunch of the inmates showed up at the curio shop.

They said, "We want you to play on our fast-pitch softball team."

"No," I said.

"Why not?" they asked.

"There's a jacket on me," I said. "If the jacket is really lifted and I don't ever have to hear about it again, I might play on the team."

"It's done," they said. "We will deal with the guys who have been bothering you."

After that the jacket was lifted and I played on a fast pitch softball team. I never had another threatening letter on my bed or received a comment on the matter. Some of my accusers were even on the softball team and did not bring up the subject. God used my past in baseball to grant me favor in the eyes of the inmates and to protect me. Here I was gaining the respect of all the inmates. God was turning things around for me. For some reason He wanted me to play softball.

During my time at Pine Lodge, I met a prison chaplain named Walt Shipley. He was a very sincere Christian man. Walt was very honest about his own life and knew about the Fellowship and me. We developed a good friendship. One day he told me that the Lord would fully heal my life and bring full restoration to ministry. I appreciated his telling me of the healing, but ministry was not a consideration. I wanted to get home, and make up to Terri and the children for my bad decisions.

Walt would say, "Jeff, you fell off the horse. In the future you will have to get back in the saddle and ride again."

One day, Walt Shipley's assistant informed me that an inmate who had made a threat against me had been out of prison for a few weeks. He had been in a terrible car accident and was in a coma at the hospital.

To my surprise the Chaplain assistant said, "How would you like to go and visit this guy in the hospital?"

He got special permission for me to be released out of our low security prison and to visit this guy that evening. When we arrived, he was on a special contraption and it was rotating him. His eyes were open, but I am not sure what he could understand. He could not communicate. I told him that day about Jesus' love and forgiveness for our sins.

After a few months, I was transferred to the pre-release. The pre-release was a place where you could study computers and gain other skills. This was an extra minimum-security place where you stay for about one or two months, in preparation of going to work release. After a month in the pre-release, I was allowed to move on to work release.

With six months left on my sentence, I was first sent to live in a halfway house in Spokane, Washington. All you had to do was report where you were working and write down your hours. They would confirm that you were at your place of employment by calling your employer. Who wanted to hang around a halfway house? I would get up at six every morning and work until ten at night. I was working for John Oakley at his restaurant. Every Sunday I would attend his church.

I spent a lot of time with John Oakley and Steve Bush. They ministered the Lord's love and mercy to me. They would say that the Lord is going to heal my life and use me in ministry in the future. This was appreciated and kind on their part, but I was still not thinking about ministry. We would have biblical discussions and times of prayer after the restaurant closed each night.

Working as a waiter at the restaurant, I was allowed to keep the tips, send some money home

It was a beautiful place to be in the midst of a fierce storm.

to Terri, and pay my portion of the halfway house rent. Christians in the area who knew about my situation would come and visit me at the restaurant. They heard that God had delivered me from the deception I'd lived under. One man used to come in regularly. One night he gave me a $100 tip. He came in for lunch the next day and gave me a $50 tip. I believe God put in his heart that I needed help. I immediately sent this home to Terri to help her with the bills.

When it was time for me to be released, John Oakley and other members of the church I was attending threw a big party for me. Attending New Covenant Church, and John and Steve's church I learned a lot about God's love, and really enjoyed the gentle spirit in both places. The worship and praise were pretty good as well.

During the six months I worked at the restaurant, I turned $2,400 in tips over to John Oakley. After the party at John's he gave me a check for $2,400.

"Here," he said as he handed me the envelope. "This is all the tip money you gave me."

"Steve, that money was for rent and food," I responded.

He just smiled, and said, "This is your money. I bless you in the name of the Lord. Go home and start a new life for yourself."

Later, John sold his businesses and became a pastor in Washington State.

For the word of God is living and active.
Sharper than any double-edged sword,
it penetrates even to dividing the soul and spirit, joints and marrow;
it judges the thoughts and attitudes of the heart.
(Hebrews 4:12 NIV)

Chapter 13:

Home Safe

M ay 9, 1990, I was released. It was time for me to return home. I put on new clothes—Levi Dockers pants and shirt with a pair of suspenders. Getting off the plane was an emotional time as I saw Terri, Melissa, Joseph, and Benjamin. Benjamin was now about three years old. I don't know if he exactly knew who I was. I was so grateful to see them. The Lord returned me safely to my family just as Toby had said.

Toby and Rita were also at the airport, and it was also good to see them. They are some of the kindest people on the face of the earth. Not only did they help us financially, but also they provided Terri and me with wisdom and guidance during the difficult time we walked through.

Toby suggested that Terri and I take a week at the beach, but we did not have the money to do that. I felt so bad for not being there for Terri and the children that it was hard for me to just come home and relax. Terri had done a miraculous job in saving some money during my time away. She is a very thrifty person, but I was anxious to do a résumé and get a job as soon as possible.

Our family was still living in the small two-bedroom apartment on Pritchard Avenue in Chapel Hill, North Carolina. The children were now sixteen months older, and Melissa needed her own room. The boys had bunk beds and Melissa had a single bed. Their small room was getting a little tight.

On the first Sunday back, we decided to attend Christian Assembly Church. Paul Gordon and the church had been so gracious to our family and me. It was so nice to just sit with my family and be among friends. The worship was beautiful. It was good to be home.

Having lunch with Paul, I spoke to him about my remorse over what had taken place in the Fellowship. I knew the Lord had forgiven me, but I also felt that I had destroyed the ministry that I had been in. Paul just smiled and said that I had not been in true Christian ministry. He said that the Lord would bring a full restoration, and place me back into a ministry in the future that would be led by and glorify Him. This was hard to comprehend at the time; all I could see was the damage I had done.

Paul shared with me some very good advice, "Jeff, the Lord forgives you, I forgive you, your wife and children forgive you as well. You need to forgive yourself. You do not have to live in the past or talk about the bad decisions. Make it a point to not feel obligated to speak about your bad decisions anymore; you are forgiven and unless it is purposeful, hold your peace on this matter."

One day, people were praying for me at Christian Assembly Church and a lady came up to me with a word of encouragement.

She said, "In times past, you were putting bad seeds into the ground, so God took a sickle and mowed them all down. As you continue to turn to Him, He is going to give you good seed. There will be a life of fruitfulness. You have experienced the correction of God and now you will experience the goodness of God."

It was miraculous that the Lord had brought us to a place where my sin would not be staring me in the face every day. I do not know why the Lord had chosen to show me such mercy, but I am grateful for it.

New Life, New Job

In the next few weeks, I was introduced to Don and Barbara Levine, who were the owners of the Potted Plant. They offered me a job on their outdoor landscape crew for minimum wage. It actually felt good to begin working manual labor. The job consisted of outdoor landscaping, indoor maintenance of plants, and working at their greenhouse.

They were very nice people who also came from a Jewish heritage. I had told them all about my past in my interview with them. They were very understanding and told me they had no problem hiring me because Toby Kahr had recommended me.

As their business had grown over the years, their employees had neglected some of the dif-ferent segments. Don and Barbara told me how hard it was to get good employees. I explained how I could help them clean up various aspects of their business, and they gave me the go ahead to do this. In a few months they were so pleased with my efforts, they put me on a salary and put me over all aspects with them being over me. I was in a better position to see what I really wanted to do.

They reminded me that we have all made mistakes in life.

My brother, Rick, asked me if I wanted to begin a vending company business with him. I went to Pepsi Cola to see if this was possible, and they said, *"Yes."* I continued to work for the Potted Plant four days a week, and I worked for my own company, called Tar Heel Vending, Inc., and Rick on the other days. We put Pepsi machines in businesses from Chapel Hill all the way to Raleigh. Pepsi supplied me with machines if we would provide the snacks and only sell Pepsi products. This seemed simple enough. Within about six months, we had about thirty locations in place, and our vending business was beginning to build and prosper.

After working for Don and Barbara for about nine months, Don and I had lunch together. Don asked me how I liked the job, and if I could see myself doing this indefinitely. I told Don that I wanted to develop my vending business into a full time job. About six months later, I had a meeting with the Pepsi Company and was told they were going to change their strategies. I would not be able to have unlimited Pepsi vending machines anymore. I saw the writing on the wall, and we entered into a new agreement for the machines that were already in place. I would return the machines to them in exchange for royalties on sales in those locations.

Now instead of having two jobs, I had no job and the royalties would be minimal. I went to Terri and let her know what had taken place, and she recommended that I speak with Toby Kahr, who was the Vice President of Human Resources at Duke University. Toby advised me to come to Duke and apply with their temporary services.

Toby became a real father figure to me. I would watch Toby come home from work at Duke University and polish his shoes a certain way. He would speak with me about integrity in the work place and with God. He encouraged me to always be honest and never cut corners. He gave me the correction that I needed. He told me he loved me dearly, and he and Rita only wanted what was best for the children and us. Toby and Rita not only told me what needed correction, but what they saw in my future.

Toby said once, "Jeff, you are a born leader."

I turned to Rita and said, "I let God down and no longer want to be a leader."

She chuckled, and replied, "Then you're ready to learn to lead now."

Toby and Rita were not only good counselors, but also encouragers. They taught me how to be a husband and father, not only by what they said, but also by what I saw in their lives. One of Toby's greatest strengths was that, with all his accomplishments, he was gentle. He did not have to raise his voice to get his point across. He and Rita were full of wisdom that they put into practice.

To this day, I call them once a week to check in and speak about the week and pray together. I have made myself accountable to them, and over the years, though they will always have my respect as my Christian parents, they treat me as an equal. As we have gotten older, the relationship has somewhat changed, as has that with our own children.

Reflection!

Looking back, when Terri and I were in the Fellowship, we only received counsel from the people in that group. It is very dangerous for anyone to only receive advice from people in one church or setting. I realized that while Terri and I were in the cult, Christians from the outside were trying to give us good advice.

People who were Christians and not connected to us in any way, were all saying similar things: "This group is heading the wrong way and here is why."

Even people who were not Christians were giving us good advice, yet at the time we were under a bad influence. Therefore, I was also a bad influence on others. I was an instrument of Satan and did not realize it.

I failed because I did not listen to the multitude of counsel available outside my regular circle of friends within our little group. Now, I have friends all over the country and world to whom I can go for good advice. I read God's Word daily and do not get in a hurry with decisions. I would like to encourage people in churches to look beyond their individual denominations and small group of friends and receive from a multitude of counselors.

Where there is no counsel, the people fall;
but in the multitude of counselors there is safety.
(Proverbs 11:14 NKJV)

Chapter 14:

That's a God Thing!

———————◆———————

One Sunday, Terri, the kids, and I went to Christian Assembly Church. We had a special speaker, who was a Jewish Evangelist, named Bobby Martz. He gave a great message of encouragement to the church that morning, and then he encouraged people to come forward if they had any prayer needs or a physical ailment that needed prayer as well.

I had a bad injury to my right knee. There was pain, a clicking noise, and at times when I lifted heavy things, my right knee would give out. I decided that I would go forward and have prayer for my knee. As I proceeded up the aisle to the front, warmth went from the top of my head, down my body, through my knee, to my toes. I stopped mid-aisle and was stomping my knee on the ground. It was healed. I hadn't even made it to the front. I was in shock.

As I walked forward, Mr. Martz pointed to me and said, "Why have you come forward? You have already received what you asked for!"

He continued, "Thus saith the Lord: in times past you did not have favor with God or man, but in the days ahead, you will now have favor with God and man. There will be times when you come into impossible circumstances with man, but they are not impossible for the Lord. The Lord will make possible that which is impossible with man for you."

Then he said that he saw me in a vision with a big smile. He said that as time would go on, I would fall in love with Jesus and enter into greater joy!

Within a few weeks, I had been given a six-week assignment with the Environmental Services Department for Duke University. At my interview, my manager, Larry Bradley, explained that I should not expect to have employment beyond the six weeks and also to not expect this to lead to anything further. He hired me and assigned me to a facility that they were having trouble keeping clean. Good employees were hard to find, he shared. I was assigned to Duke Diet and Fitness Center.

Each day, I had to clean the bathrooms, the carpeting in the hallways and the athletic equipment in the fitness center. Duke Diet and Fitness Center had some famous people come to learn how to manage their weight. During my time there, the wife of Dick Van Dyke was there to lose weight. When I was cleaning the treadmills and weight equipment, she asked me how to use the machines. I explained to her that I would get her an instructor. Being a physical education graduate and knowing how to use the machines, it was hard to take a back seat.

I also met Dennis Scott, who was six feet eight inches tall, and played with the Orlando Magic pro basketball team. He was looking to lose a few pounds and get in shape. Every day at lunch, I would go to the basketball court and play one on one with Dennis. He was a good guy and had a good sense of humor.

One day as we were going to play, he turned to me and said, "Accept my apologies in advance for what I am going to do to you."

In a game of "Twenty-one," I beat him 21-18. He was in shock, as he is a full foot taller than me. In the game of one on one, you can keep getting the ball back if you keep making baskets. He was a little embarrassed, but we had fun together. One day, he asked me if I would pray for his knees as he was having a little trouble with them and was taking some physical therapy.

I kept working hard at my job, making $5.80 per hour. This was not enough to pay all of our bills, but I did not tell anyone this. Sometimes, I would go to our mailbox and find cash or checks from friends made out to Terri and me. It was incredible. Sometimes, there would be an envelope with cash with no name on it. The Lord was providing me with a job, and making up the difference that my job was not providing for. Our friend, Rita Kahr, would buy a lot of canned goods in bulk. She would actually take a permanent marker and put the purchase dates on them. Goods in cans have a long shelf life, and we would gladly often be the recipients of many cans of food with older dates on them.

Toby and Rita have always been very generous people. They always cared about people and are true examples of parents and

The Lord was showing me, He provides.

Christians. God used them mightily in our lives.

It was tough and humbling that I had a bachelor's degree in physical education and was making $5.80 an hour. I was really trying to find proper employment that fit my ability and skill set, but I needed to be patient and see what was available. Each day I would look at the classifieds for job openings and sent out hundreds of résumés but was not having a lot of success.

One day as I was vacuuming, I prayed, "Lord, have You lost track of me? I am doing all that I know to do. I am working hard, sending out resumes and desire to take good care of Terri and the kids."

I asked the Lord if mopping floors was important to Him. All of a sudden a Bible verse came to me from Proverbs 22:29, "Do you see a man who excels in his work? He will stand before kings: He will not stand before unknown men" (NKJV). I thought to myself, *am I losing my mind or is the Lord speaking to me through these passages?* I decided to be the best worker that I knew to be. I thought to myself, *does the Lord really take interest in the smallest unseen things that I do?* I was of the opinion that He did, and that little unseen things are very important to Him, like mopping floors, and people who screw up in life and are sincerely sorry for their past actions.

I was determined to show God an attitude of gratefulness, and do the best job I knew to do.

A few days later, my manager, Larry Bradley, came to Duke Diet and Fitness Center dressed to the max in a suit and suspenders. Larry was an ex-military officer. His shoes were shined and he was there to walk with me and inspect the facility.

When we were done, he said, "Jeff, the place has never looked better."

I had pulled together the other employees, and we worked together as a team. Larry recognized that there was now a sense of order and cleanliness. Larry was a good example to me. He had a kind way with the employees who worked for him. When he needed to speak with employees in problem situations, he always had a special phrase: *Throw some honey on the situation!*

Larry brought to my attention that his boss, the Executive Director of Environmental Services for Duke University, would be coming next week to do a formal inspection of the whole facility. Larry asked me if I could take the lead and have it looking good for his boss. On the day he came with his boss and inspected the center for cleanliness, I wanted him to look good before his boss, so I went to a different area of the facility. Somehow, they found me cleaning some athletic equipment. Larry, again dressed to the max, introduced me to his boss, Bob Linehart.

Bob extended his hand to me, "Jeff, my name is Bob Linehart. I am the Executive Director for Duke University Environmental Services. Larry tells me you are from Chicago. I am from Chicago, too! What is it you really want to do with your life?"

I said, "Bob, I desire to work in the field of management."

Bob asked me If I had a résumé with me and I said, *"Yes."*

I went to my car, where I had multiple copies, and gave him one. It was a Thursday, and he asked me if I could come to his office on Monday.

On the following Monday, I went to meet Bob in his office at Duke. Bob was a man in his early thirties and very bright. He explained to me that he worked for a contract management company, called ServiceMaster, with corporate headquarters in Downers Grove, Illinois. He said it was a multi-billion dollar international company that specializes in managing custodial contracts in hospitals, food services, plant operations, clinical engineering, and owns many other recognized companies.

"Jeff," he explained, "would you have an interest in working for ServiceMaster, and would you be willing to relocate your family?"

"I am certainly open to the idea," I replied.

He further explained that his company would pay for expenses of relocation for a management position. He told me that they have great training and educational opportunities. ServiceMaster was founded by a man named Marion Wade, who was a Christian and built the company on four Christian Principles:

1) To honor God in all that we do.
2) To help people develop.
3) To pursue excellence.
4) To grow profitably.

These objectives are the core values of this corporation, and would also become pillars in the new foundations of my life.

I really liked what I was hearing and filled out an application with Bob. It had a section for criminal background, so I immediately told him about my past. He explained to me that if I had proper references, he felt his company would be willing to give me a chance. It would be up to me to make good on this opportunity. Bob Linehart was a Christian and very kind in helping me in the next step that would take place in about six months.

Life Goes On

I had now been home for about a year and a half. Melissa and Joseph were going to Estes Hills Elementary School in Chapel Hill. They were doing very well in school and making friends. Terri was much happier with me at home and was able to continue as a stay at home mom, doing school projects with Melissa and Joseph, attending to Benjamin and volunteering in the community.

Terri and I continued in fellowship with Toby, Rita, and friends at Christian Assembly. Paul Gordon had a friend named, Jerry Daley, who was the pastor of Grace Church which was also a very wonderful group of Christian people. Grace Church was much closer to our home. Jerry knew our background and was also committed to our healing from past events. We made additional friendships and enjoyed going to this church as we maintained our friendships at Christian Assembly.

A friend at Christian Assembly bought an Italian restaurant and hired his son-in-law, Vinnie, to be the head chef and manager. They called me and said that they wanted me to come and consult with their business for about a week as they were having problems with cash flow and food costs.

He knew that Vinnie was a great chef, but was not sure that he was managing efficiently. A Jewish accountant friend, who understood the restaurant business, helped me understand that Vinnie was using the highest quality ingredients in his recipes, but not charging enough for the entrees. He would either have to find lower cost ingredients or raise his prices. My friends appreciated my input and help, and I believe Vinnie began to do better at managing their business.

I was now working in a new department at Duke in Medical Records when I received an additional application from ServiceMaster at my home. I was wondering what this was about and called Bob Linehart. He explained a man named, Ben Pearsall, wanted to interview me for a position in Orangeburg, South Carolina, as an assistant manager in environmental services with a workforce of forty people. Bob arranged for me to meet with Ben in Winston Salem, N.C., at a hospital that had ServiceMaster management in place. Ben Pearsall, an area manager for ServiceMaster, was over a large area of hospitals in North and South Carolina.

Ben interviewed me and it went very similar to my interview with Bob Linehart. He was a good Christian man and wanted to know if I would be interested in taking a position in Orangeburg at the Regional Medical Center as the assistant manager for Environmental Services.

We discussed my past and Ben told me, "Jeff, you paid your debt to society. If I can confirm what you are saying with Toby Kahr, there is no reason we can't offer you this position."

After confirmation from Toby and additional references from the Levine's, I was offered this job on April 6, 1992. My beginning salary for the assistant manager's job was $22,800. ServiceMaster agreed to move us to West Columbia, S.C., a thirty-five minute drive from my job in Orangeburg. Terri and I decided that we would have better schools for our children in West Columbia. Melissa and Joseph were in school and

Benjamin was in kindergarten for half a day. Terri babysat for a little girl and continued as a stay at home mom. During our time in West Columbia, Melissa and Joseph began to play soccer, baseball, softball, and basketball. Our children loved sports and they excelled in school. We lived at an apartment complex called Quail Hollow with a nice swimming pool.

ServiceMaster had some great management training programs and sent me to Chicago for a few weeks of company training. I was in charge of a crew of forty employees along with a day and evening supervisor. My boss, Stuart Spurlin, was a round, funny guy who was always looking to play jokes on the employees.

Part of our responsibilities was to strip floors and apply new finish. In addition, we had special machines to clean carpets. To see if there was any excess moisture in the carpet after doing a full extraction, we had a moisture stick with two prongs on the end. All you had to do was turn on the switch and put the prongs in the carpet. The stick made a crackling noise if there was moisture still in it, and the louder it got the more moisture there was.

One day when I came into Stu's office, he pulled out the stick and explained to me how it worked. This was his new toy. He explained that the stick could detect moisture on anything. He told me to put the prongs against a wall. There was no sound because there was no moisture. Then he told me to put the prongs on my arm. The stick began to make the crackling noise. It almost sounded like a Geiger counter that detects radiation.

"Pretty cool," I remarked.

Stu made up his mind to play a joke on one of our carpet and flooring guys. He knew that this guy, Albert, had never seen the moisture stick. Stu called Albert on his pager and told him to report to his office.

Stu said to Albert, "We have had a leakage of radioactivity from the x-ray area and you have been stripping floors there. It is mandatory that we do a radiation check on you immediately. If we find radioactivity, we must take you to the back dock and hose you off."

Stu showed Albert how putting the stick on the wall, it made no sound. Then he put it on Albert's arm and then face. The stick made a lot of noise and Albert freaked. I thought he was going to wet his pants. Albert screamed and ran out of the room.

"Stu," I said, "I think you went too far this time."

He was in stitches, but Albert was on the way to the hospital's vice president's office. He thought he was really radioactive. Stu had some explaining to do to Brenda, the VP we reported to, but I must admit there was never a dull moment working for Stu.

A Jewish Christian Who Eats Pork?

At this hospital each day at 6:45 a.m., the chaplain of the hospital did a moment of prayer over the loud speaker. We now lived in the South, "The Bible Belt," and things were a little more open than when we lived in the north. It was nice to hear public prayers in our hospital. People were not shy about making it known that they were Christians or what church they attended. One of my supervisors, Shelly, a very sweet African-American woman, came to me one morning and caught me by surprise.

She said, "Jeff, I discern that you are a man of the cloth. Would it be okay if before the morning hospital prayer that our first shift employees come into your office and have a time of prayer for our staff?"

I told Shelly that I would have to speak with Mr. Spurlin and see if this would be possible. Stuart said it would be okay as long as it was not mandatory. I made it clear to the employees that anyone could come, but I would not be the leader of the prayer meeting. This is something we would do together and anyone could pray. We actually saw some good fruit from our times together as people would come in with different kinds of prayer requests. It really unified our morning staff. People would come to me with their problems and visit with me in my office. I always tried to be a good listener and see what I could do to help.

At times during my stay in Orangeburg, I felt like a missionary to that area. The culture was a lot different than the north and even some more modern southern cities. Orangeburg was a city where a lot of marches took place in the 1960s during the days of Martin Luther King Jr.. Everyone got along at the hospital, but blacks and whites were more separate than in most places I had been. There were white neighborhoods and black neighborhoods. There were white churches and black churches.

One time we decided to have an employee cookout. The man in charge of our pharmacy in the hospital, Rodgers Jarvis, had a quartet called the Jarvis Brothers. They could sing some beautiful black gospel. They agreed to come to our cookout and perform at no cost for our employees. They did all their songs for us and were a big hit with our employees. I found out later that they had performed at the Apollo Theater in New York, did a great job, and were a hit with the audience.

Jarvis came to visit me one day at my office. The word had gotten around that I was a Jewish Christian. He asked me if I would come and share my testimony at his Sunday school at the largest black church in Orangeburg in a few weeks. I said sure and later mentioned this to Stu. Stu said that this was not done in these parts. A white preacher would never minister in a black church. He said it could cause me some problems. I explained to Stu that this was wrong and I would encourage people wherever I was welcome to speak.

When the day came for me to visit Jarvis' church, I went with Terri and our children. In we walked; the only white faces in the place. Worship began and the place rocked. The worship music was some of the best I had heard in a long time. Even the Jarvis brothers sang a song. We were made to feel welcome and at Sunday school my testimony was well received.

One day at lunch, Stu brought me to a barbecue house. He ordered me a plate of pork, white rice with yellow hash, and coleslaw. It was the first time I had eaten hash. Another day he took me to a slaughterhouse and purchased a bag of pig parts for making hash. This included the snout, ears, tongue, etc. This stuff apparently finds its way into hotdogs and other foods as well he told me. Stu insisted that I bring it home and have Terri make a pot of hash. Upon my arrival at home, Terri took out the camera and took pictures of Joseph, Melissa, and Ben who were curiously investigating the contents of the bag. Terri actually made over a gallon of hash, which I brought to work at one of our employee parties.

Stu thought this was intriguing and called the chaplain of the hospital to visit me one morning. He introduced me as a Jew who ate pork barbecue. I did not grow up eating a lot of pork products but, for the sake of making my friends feel comfortable, I ate this after giving thanks. Stu was determined to introduce me to other southern foods, so he took me for "bald" peanuts, actually called "boiled peanuts." They were hot and pretty tasty.

Continuing My Education

After about one year of working in Orangeburg, I heard from my brother, Rick, that my mom's brother, Jerry, was sick with cancer. I called Uncle Jerry to see how he was doing. I had not spoken with him in twenty-five years. He was living in California in the city of San Juan Capistrano.

The day I spoke with him, he said that he had been thinking about me and wondering how I was doing. Uncle Jerry actually became a believer in Jesus before I did and on this phone conversation he explained to me how he got saved. During the course of our conversation, it came up about me

189

furthering my education. I told Uncle Jerry I had found a Master's Degree Program in Management of Organizations in Columbia, S.C, a satellite program of Southern Wesleyan University.

"You must start the program as soon as possible," he told me.

"I need to work for ServiceMaster a few years more before I am eligible for reimbursement for school," I explained.

"Jeff, you need to start now!" he insisted.

I explained, "As much as I want to do this, I do not have the means to get started. It would cost about $10,000."

About a week later I found a check in our mailbox for $13,000 for my education and extras. I was floored! I called him to thank him for his generous gift. Over the next three years we grew very close. He moved to Florida to be closer to my mom. My mom really respected him and he was able to share his faith in Jesus Christ with her. She really listened and let him pray for her at times.

During our time in West Columbia, we attended North Side Baptist Church. The pastor, Bill Cloud, was a wonderful preacher and a good man. One day he invited, Ricky Stanley, the step-brother of Elvis Presley, to speak. He shared his testimony and during the altar call our son, Joseph, who was about nine years old at the time, went forward to accept Jesus, fully understanding what he was doing.

Melissa became good friends with Pastor Cloud's daughter. One thing they had in common was their love for horses and riding. Her friend's family had horses and a large pasture where they would sometimes go riding together.

Melissa regularly attended the weekly youth meetings at the church and on one particular evening came home full of excitement saying, "Guess what mom!" Terri answered, "You gave your heart to Jesus tonight!"

Melissa said, "Yes!" Terri and I were very happy about Melissa's decision to follow Jesus. Melissa was about eleven years.

This same evening Benjamin, after having witnessed Melissa's announcement, came to Terri and me and said, "I want Jesus in my heart now, too."

We were wondering if he was just doing this because Melissa had come home with this news, but he kept insisting that Terri and I pray with him. At bedtime, we knelt beside Ben's bed and he invited Jesus in his heart. I asked the Lord to show me his heart so that I would know if he understood what he had done. Terri and I left the room leaving a little light on as we always did because Ben was afraid of the dark.

Ben said, "Mom, I don't need the light on any more. Jesus is in my heart. I am not afraid anymore."

At five years old, he never requested that the light be left on again. I was beginning to see the Lord's hand in restoring the lost years in the Fellowship. He was making up for eight years of sin and deception.

Promotion Comes From the Lord

Around August of 1993, Ben Pearsall, came to do an inspection of the cleanliness of our hospital. He seemed very pleased, and told me that he had received a call from Charlotte, N.C., from an area manager named, Jim Cheek. Jim wanted to know if I was interested in moving to Charlotte to work at Carolina Medical Center as the second and third shift manager in charge of eighty-five employees with supervisors and managers who would report directly to me. Terri and I prayed about this and we felt that this promotion was good for our family. I had taken two classes from Southern Wesleyan University; so I spoke with Uncle Jerry who also said the promotion was a good thing and suggested I inquire about school in Charlotte.

Terri, the children, and I moved to a suburb of Charlotte called Indian Trail. ServiceMaster now increased my salary to $26,000 per year. We moved into a three-bedroom house on Red Lantern Road. Benjamin was now six, so with the children in school all day Terri was able to get a job outside the home. Terri's additional income working in a local elementary school cafeteria was very helpful.

As I was finishing my employment in Orangeburg, I had heard of a baseball league called the Men's Senior Baseball League. I decided to play on a men's team in West Columbia called the West Columbia Yankees. I had a pretty good year as a batter and pitcher. I was now thirty-eight years old. The team that won the league championship, the Columbia Braves, was going to Clearwater, Florida, for a National Tournament. They asked me to come as a relief pitcher. Our team ended up in the National MSBL Championship game against a team from Puerto Rico. There was a guy on our team, Craig, who wore a practice uniform with the word *Doyle* on it. I asked Craig about that. Craig said that he was getting ready to invite me to something that was more fun that playing baseball.

Do you see a man who excels in his work?
He will stand before kings: He will not stand before unknown men.
(Proverbs 22:29 NKJV)

Chapter 15:

Back to Baseball

After I moved to Charlotte, Craig called me and invited me to a training session for the Doyle Baseball School out of Winter Haven, Florida. I met, Blake Doyle, the brother of Denny and Brian, who were all professional players. Blake played in Triple A with Baltimore and Cincinnati. Brian was the World Series leading hitter for the 1978 Yankees, and Denny had a twelve-year career with the Phillies, California Angels, and Boston Red Sox (World Series 1975).

When I went to their professional instructional session, I realized that they ran a Christian-based baseball academy. Through Craig, I was invited to become a professional instructor with the Doyle School of Baseball in the spring of 1993. My responsibilities would be to teach children around the country how to the play the game of baseball, conduct anti-drug and alcohol sessions, and lead chapel services.

For doing something that I enjoyed—teaching baseball to children six to eighteen years old, the Doyles paid their instructors a fair wage for their time away from their families on Saturdays and Sundays. I was able to take all my children with me at times. I was working with ServiceMaster and now I had a part-time seasonal job. Terri was still working in the school system as a baker.

I liked my new job in Charlotte at the Carolina Medical Center with ServiceMaster. I had a lot of responsibility on second and third shift. It took an adjustment for me with my sleep habits as I was used to getting up early and going to bed at 11:00 p.m. Now, I reported for work at 2:00 p.m. and got home at 12:00-1:00 a.m. When I got home at night, Terri and the children were already in bed. I purposely worked very hard, so that I could put myself in position for a promotion and get back on a first shift schedule.

In the fall of 1994, I was asked to move again and take a promotion as the Director for Environmental Services at Baptist Medical Center in Easley, South Carolina. I would work first shift, be in charge of forty employees, and be paid much more. I was given a raise to move with all expenses paid.

We found a nice, little home in Liberty, S.C. for rent. My children went to Liberty Elementary, Middle and High Schools. Terri obtained employment with the Pickens County DSS as a social worker, and I continued with the Doyle School of Baseball.

We went to church at Liberty First Baptist. The senior pastor, Joe Hayes, and I became good friends. He asked me if I would share my personal testimony in church on how I got saved as a Jew. This went really well and I became very close with Joe and our church. I also became very close with, Brian and Connie Doyle, of the Doyle School of Baseball. I would take our family to Winter Haven, Florida, and celebrate Christmas with the Doyle's being part of a Holiday Baseball School.

Brian loved to do the chapel sessions for up to 300 children and parents. Many times, I heard him do an Old Testament devotional, and then do an altar call. Brian was a gifted evangelist and we would see many children and sometimes parents give their lives to Jesus. I told my pastor about Brian and his gift of sharing Christ with children and adults through baseball. Joe asked me if Brain would come to Liberty First Baptist Church and do a youth rally. He could speak in schools, at the local Fellowship of Christian Athletes at Clemson University, and at our hospital. Brian liked this idea and came with Connie. Many came to Christ. It was a special time for us and our community, and a time for Brian and Connie to stay on a scenic property with a quaint mill and get some rest among friends.

It so happened that Southern Wesleyan University was just a few miles from our house. In the spring of 1995, I went back to school on the main campus. My company also decided to help pay for me to finish my master's degree. With the money that Uncle Jerry gave me, I was able to make a down payment on a home a few blocks away. We purchased a nice brick home, about 2400 square feet, with an outdoor in-ground swimming pool. Our family loved our new home with three bedrooms upstairs. Each child now had their own bedroom. Terri and I had the downstairs to ourselves.

About that same time, Joe Hicks, the lead instructor in charge of a baseball school in Danville, Virginia, asked me for my help. He asked me to come, instruct, and to lead the chapel service. We had 112 students sign up for the school. The Sunday chapel was at 1:00 p.m. and 175 people came! We usually had about twenty-four to forty participants on the average. This was extraordinary!

That day I did a devotional on the "Storms of Life" from Mark 4:35-41. When I finished, I asked the parents and children if they wanted Jesus in their hearts. Forty parents and children raised their hands, prayed to be saved, and invited Christ to be their Lord and Savior. Wow! I had never experienced anything like this in my life. I not only saw children invite Christ into their hearts, but parents as well.

I was thinking to myself that there was not going to be any church follow-up as this program was not working with any local churches. I went to Brian and spoke with him about what happened. He said he was getting goose bumps as I was sharing how people gave their lives to Jesus. New believers need a good church and follow up, so the question was, how could we do this?

I began to think that I would like to develop a national and international program where no child would ever have to pay for baseball instruction. The importance of this type of outreach would be to share Christ with parents and children. We could connect children and families to the local church using baseball as a platform. My focus would be young people as they are the future of the nations.

If you work with the children and get them involved in good churches, then the parents will see the value of this investment in their child's life.

By making young people the focus of our ministry, then there is a good chance that their parents will also join the church and become believers in Jesus. My desire was to work with good churches and Christian businesses to develop partnerships in communities to bring the gospel message, discipleship programs, and humanitarian aid. New ideas were developing for the future, but how could I accomplish this and raise funds for a dream that the Lord had placed in my heart?

In the fall of 1996, I graduated with my master's degree in Management of Organizations from Southern Wesleyan University. In the spring of 1997, my pastor, Joe Hayes, showed me a video of a sports evangelistic organization called, International Sports Federation. We watched this together and I was impressed with how they used multiple sports as a platform to share their faith. Joe gave me the telephone number of Cheryl

Wolfinger, the president, and encouraged me to call her. We both felt that the Lord may be developing a relationship with their organization.

I called Cheryl later that week, and she agreed that the Lord was getting ready to use me internationally in baseball evangelism. We prayed together to know the Lord's will and the next steps. A few weeks later, Cheryl called me and asked if I would be interested in leading a team of ten to fifteen instructors to a place called Cloppenburg, Germany. This is located in northwest Germany. After additional prayer and speaking with Terri, we agreed that in May 1997, I would go to Germany.

This was an incredible opportunity to visit the area of the Holocaust. I had forgiven German people for what had happened, but to go to the very areas where it had occurred was something else. Could the Lord have some purpose using baseball to bring me to Germany?

A few weeks after I had agreed to go to Germany, Marty Clary, who pitched with the Atlanta Braves from 1987 to 1990, came to share his personal testimony with our youth in my church. Terri and our children heard him speak but I was home that Sunday afternoon. Terri called me immediately and told me that Marty wanted to meet me. I told Terri that I was tired and wanted to relax as it was a Sunday and my day off.

She answered, "You better get over here right now as I believe that the Lord is in on this. Marty is waiting for you to come."

I quickly went over to the church and met Marty. He had pitched in the Big Ten Conference for Northwestern, one of our rival schools. I was just a few years older than Marty. He was from the Detroit suburbs and I was from Chicago. We had a lot in common. Terri told him that I was a Jewish believer and a professional instructor with the Doyle School of Baseball. Marty told me that they were doing a baseball program that weekend with a local church led by Pastor Greg Sweet. The baseball program was called, "More than Conquerors." Greg had invited Marty, Jose

Alvarez, who also pitched with the Braves, players from the Greenville Braves Double A team and their head coach to participate.

Marty invited me to come and do the fielding station with them at the baseball clinic and to meet Jose Alvarez and Greg Sweet. On this April spring day, we had over 300 children and about 200 parents and other guests. Jose asked the coach of the Greenville Braves, Marty, and I to share a short testimony. He told me to take ten minutes and share how I got saved as a Jew. Jose did the altar call that day, and many made professions of faith and invited Jesus in their hearts.

A few weeks later, I went with International Sports Federation to Germany. I remember the first night arriving in Cloppenberg. Our host, Pastor Stephen Jett, took us to a steak barbecue at someone's home. We had T- bones, pork steaks, potato salad, and additional German food. After dinner, Stephen turned to forty or so people who were invited from his church and said that Jeff is a "Yuden" Christian, which means Jeff, is a Jewish Christian. The guests seemed a little stunned. How did this happen some asked? Steve asked me to briefly share my testimony. As I finished, I saw tears streaming out of people's eyes.

When the evening was over, my host, Henry Fennen, in whose home I would stay, started his Volkswagen toward his residence. The next thing I knew, he was taking me by a few churches. Then we stopped in front of an iron gate that had a Jewish Star on it. We walked past the gate and there was a Jewish cemetery and a grassy area, which used to have a synagogue on it. It was burned to the ground at the beginning of the Holocaust on Kristallnacht, called the "night of broken glass." It was a day when the German people ransacked the Jewish people. They broke the windows of businesses, burned synagogues to the ground, vandalized homes and that was just the beginning of their woes. I broke down and fell on the ground crying. The Lord brought me to Germany for more than teaching baseball.

There was something more that He wanted me to see. Henry put his arm around me and, in his broken English, we just prayed and wept together.

Our baseball clinics went well; some of my supporters of this trip encouraged me to stay for a few extra days and tour Germany. Henry also wanted to do this with me and we decided to go to a concentration camp called Bergen Belsen. On our way to Bergen Belsen, we stopped off in a beautiful city called Celle. It was close to Bergen Belsen and he had a friend who lived there. While visiting there, his friend's father, who was in his early eighties, came in the room. He explained that he was a retired fireman. This man was in great shape for his age. Henry told his friend that I was a Jewish Christian and his father overheard.

"Christ killers," his father commented.

I was in shock, but not totally surprised. He must have had corks in his ears and heard only the Jewish part. This was part of Nazi Propaganda in the '30s and '40s. Instead of getting angry or saying one word, I had a peace that surpassed all comprehension. I said to myself, *this guy looks like my grandfather. The reason he believes this stuff is the brainwashing he received during the Nazi era. He is deceived like I was in the Fellowship.* Can you imagine? The Lord's love welled up in my heart. The old man was somewhat embarrassed that this came out of his mouth. He walked out of the house, and the next thing I knew I followed him to his garden.

I said, "So, you like gardening, too."

He spoke English, so I continued, "So tell me what vegetables do you like growing?"

The next thing I knew, we were conversing and I was showing him pictures of Terri and the kids. He was quite interested. I went back into the house and now he followed me. Henry and I were ready to go.

The father of Henry's friend said to me, "Jeff, when you return to Germany and if you bring your wife, would you please come and visit with me again?"

I want to tell you God's love is more powerful that anything you can imagine. It can penetrate the stoniest heart. It can break through walls of deception.

The Lord is all-powerful and He can fight our battles.

When Henry and I arrived in Bergen Belsen, we visited the Holocaust site. Anne Frank died at Bergen Belsen less than a week before it was liberated. The museum attendants took us into a room and showed us liberation films of the Bergen Belsen concentration camp. I was in shock to see human beings who had become like living skeletons. These were my Jewish brothers and sisters who made it through alive. The others were not as lucky. Thousands of dead bodies were strewn all around the facility. What horror, and Bergen Belsen was only supposed to be a placement facility. In the liberation, the Allies took German citizens from nearby cities to show them the atrocities that had gone on in their country. They made the German soldiers gather the bodies and bury them in mass graves. Henry and I went out back where there is a memorial and we visited the mass graves. When we reached the graves where thousands of Jewish people were buried, Henry broke down and cried. We silently knelt down, prayed, and cried together.

I left Germany after ten days with a lot of new friends and an incredible education of the past. We had very good baseball clinics for children and helped Pastor Jett begin a little league program. I visited Cloppenberg one year later and helped Steve again with his baseball ministry.

A few years later, Steve moved to pastor a church in Amberg located in Bavaria between Munich and Nuremburg. Steve invited me again, and this time I came with Terri, our son Benjamin, and some of our friends. We went to visit Dachau in Munich, which was a concentration camp where Jewish people were told they were going for a shower only to be taken to poison gas chambers and to their deaths. They were then cremated in mass numbers. Can you imagine such atrocities? The human heart can be black, including my own. If we don't come to grips with the potential that we all have to do evil, it can and will happen again. History repeats itself in the individual life and in nations.

I am grateful that the Lord had intervened in my life and corrected me. That is not to say that damage wasn't done, but I am thankful for His mercy and forgiveness. The Lord has a way of using all things together for good to those who are called to His purposes (Romans 8:28).

After returning from Germany in 1997, I realized I desired to be involved in international baseball ministry. Marty Clary, and his pastor, Michael Cloer, from Siloam Baptist Church in Powdersville, S.C., came to visit me at work one day. Michael spoke in church on a series called, The Jewish Roots of the Faith. He gave me a series of eight cassette tapes. I thanked him and listened to them whenever I traveled to my baseball clinics with the Doyle Baseball School. In a few weeks I had finished the series and felt that Michael Cloer had much to teach me about the Jewish roots of the Christian Faith. They had a great International Ministry Program at Siloam Baptist Church.

I asked Terri and our children to visit Siloam with me as Marty and Michael gave us an invitation to visit anytime. After the first visit, we knew that the Lord wanted us to get more ministry experience than Liberty First Baptist could provide. They were a small country church and not as focused on international ministry. Siloam was a much larger church that was involved in worldwide outreach.

I spoke with, Joe Hayes, at Liberty First Baptist, and he understood that we wanted some additional experience in international ministry from a larger church. I explained to him that he was a great pastor and it was not because of any dissatisfaction that we wanted to transfer our membership.

During our time at Siloam Baptist Church, Marty Clary's wife, Ginger, recommended a Messianic congregation that met on Friday evenings. The pastor's name was Paul Cohen, a Jewish man. At the time, it was called Upstate Messianic Ministries and now is called, Adon Olom. Paul and I became friends, and he asked me to share my testimony in his congregation. This was before my second trip to Germany. He and some of the members of Upstate Messianic Ministries supported me in prayer and financially on my trip.

I want to take a moment to explain what it means to be a Messianic Congregation. The emphasis of a Messianic Congregation is to teach the Jewish roots of the faith and to reach the Jewish people as well as gentile believers. They meet on the Sabbath, Friday evening and Saturday morning. There is the flavor of the Jewish culture and is a congregation where Jewish people may feel more comfortable in coming to learn about Jesus from the Torah (Hebrew Scriptures) in a Jewish cultural setting.

At Upstate Messianic Ministries I met Carol and Patricia. These are very special gentile, southern ladies who have a special love for the Jewish people. They also attended Siloam Baptist Church where our family was attending on Sundays. These ladies are like big sisters to me. They encouraged Terri and me saying we would be involved in a worldwide ministry that would use baseball to the gentile nations and then Israel. They are prayer warriors that the Lord has put in my life to keep me focused on my relationship with the Lord, family life, and ministry. I am always teasing them that they are my southern mamas. They help keep me straight by giving me good sound biblical advice.

They also encouraged me that a day would come in the future when the Lord would call me to minister to my Jewish kinsmen and this would be my emphasis. In early 1998, Paul Cohen invited me to a church to hear a very unique Jewish speaker. He was an older, very distinguished man who was an Israeli war hero in the 1967 and 1973 wars. Gershon Solomon explained at the church that night how he was a paratrooper in the 1973 war and was physically there when the Israelis got back the Temple Mount. When Moshe Dayan later gave it back to the Arabs, he said the Lord had told him that someday he and his organization, The Temple Mount Faithful, would rebuild the Temple on the Temple Mount.

After Gershon spoke that night, I spent some time with him and explained to him that I was a believer in Yeshua (Jesus).

I introduced myself with my Hebrew name, Yoseph, and he said, "Yoseph, your believing in Jesus is a threat to the existence to our people."

I explained to him that I never stopped being Jewish. I was now a completed Jew and that my Jewishness meant more to me than ever. He asked me if I would be willing to speak to him at his home in Jerusalem at a future time. I accepted his invitation! We began a friendship through e-mail, and it was only a matter of time before I would go to see him in his headquarters in Jerusalem.

In 1998, when we were living in Liberty, I had some extra vacation time that I was told I had to use before the year ended. The children were in school and Terri was working. I was beginning to think that I needed to go to Israel. I asked Paul Cohen if he would go with me, as this would be a special time for both of us. It was during the Feast of Tabernacles, late in the fall of 1998. We both went and stayed in the Old City of Jerusalem at Christ Church Guest House in the Jaffa Gate. Paul and I would get up each day and walk to the Wailing Wall, the Jewish Quarters, Christian Quarters, and Arab Quarters. I loved being in the Old City and walking to the different areas with Orthodox Jews, Arabs, and people from the nations.

I had some friends living in Israel who introduced me to a man named Randy Kahn, who introduced baseball in Israel around 1985. Randy was an American-born Jew who moved to Israel from the United States. He lived in Raanana, a suburb of Tel Aviv. Randy and I really hit it off. Randy had started an organization called, The Israel Association of Baseball. He introduced me to the current president, Leon Klarfeld and David Shenker, the secretary-treasurer. They were great guys and invited me to do baseball programs in Israel. I was also introduced to Ami Baran and Bob Kessler, the vice president and president of the Israel Softball Federation. We agreed to see how we could work together in Israel through softball.

Bob Kessler and a few new friends took me to a place called Kibbutz Gezer and showed me the first little league and softball field in Israel. As you look over the left field fence, in the distance you can see the land given to King Solomon by the Pharaoh when he married his daughter. Unbelievable, baseball and softball in Israel and the holy sites! Maybe there is baseball in heaven!

One day, Paul and I went to the Wailing Wall to pray and visit.

When we walked up on the most Holy Site for the Jewish people a Rabbi, who works at the wall, came and asked us, "Are you Jewish?"

Both Paul and I said, "Yes."

He said, "I have a Hebrew prayer book called the *Siddur.* Are you familiar with it?"

Both Paul and I said, "Yes."

Paul had not gone to Hebrew school in his early years so he could not recite the prayers from the *Siddur* in Hebrew at that time. The Rabbi asked us to pray with him and after we did he proceeded to take us under the Wailing Wall to a place called the Wilson Arch. We were now in a synagogue and being led to a very old rabbi who had a Torah scroll and wanted to read with us. This rabbi asked me my family name, my father's name and then he prayed for us. Paul and I asked this old rabbi if we could pray for him and his family as well and he was thankful.

As we were walking out of the synagogue, children and adults were begging for money. I was thinking, *this is what some of my people have been reduced to.* The religious zeal of the ultraorthodox Jews, who ran the Wailing Wall and the synagogue, were there, yet they did not know the Lord, which broke my heart and caused my knees to buckle, and I began to cry.

Jesus Christ came to make it clear to the Jewish and gentile people who God is and His love for human beings. The Apostle Paul said in Romans 10:1-4,

One can know a lot about God without knowing Him in a personal way.

"Brethren, my heart's desire and prayer to God for Israel is that they might be saved. For I bear them witness that they have zeal of God, but not according to knowledge. For they being ignorant of God's righteousness, and seeking to establish their own righteousness, have not submitted to the righteousness of God. For Christ is the end of the law for righteousness to everyone who believes" (NKJV).

I met with leaders at Baptist Village in Peta Tiquiva, Israel. This place is a beautiful piece of land centrally located by Tel Aviv. They had facilities that have the ability to house 200-300 people. They were thinking of selling some of their property but asked me for some suggestions. I suggested building a baseball, softball, and sports complex with the excess land. Because of its central location it would be used by many people and be a great blessing. To my surprise they agreed and built a baseball and softball complex. The baseball field is a nice college size with grass, a sprinkler system, and lights for night games. The softball/little league field also has grass, a sprinkler system, and lights for night games.

Before leaving Israel, I had the opportunity to go to the headquarters of the Temple Mount Faithful and see Gershon Solomon. He respected me for actually coming to Israel to spend time with him. During my time in his headquarters, he showed me a few articles that would someday go into a rebuilt Temple in Jerusalem. In the year 2002, I visited with Gershon again, this time at his home in Jerusalem.

He took me a few blocks from his home and showed me two giant rocks that are the cornerstones for the Temple in the future. Yes, I saw them and they really exist. Gershon began telling me he believes he knows where the Temple Treasures are including the Ark of the Covenant. Randle Price, the author of *The Temple Treasures,* also interviewed Gershon on this subject. Gershon is a pretty interesting man! He is an orthodox Jew and he has allowed me to share about Jesus with him. We have become good friends, and he wants me to move to Israel someday. I hope that he comes to know our Jewish Messiah!

And we know that in all things God works for the good of those who love him, who have been called according to his purpose.
(Romans 8:28 NIV)

Chapter 16:

Winds of Change

In 1998, I met with my superiors from ServiceMaster. They encouraged me that I had a bright future with ServiceMaster. I was one who worked well in chaotic situations and was a good manager. I appreciated their vote of confidence but I had the strangest feeling. Why was I not more excited? Usually I am in touch with my feelings and thoughts, but not this time. All I heard in my heart was, *Go and see, Pastor Steve Ellis, at Siloam Baptist Church, and he will help you.*

After I explained my circumstances, Steve said, "Jeff, I know what's going on in your heart. The way the Lord has wired you is to be one who has the opportunity to share his faith daily. You are an evangelist, and in God's time He will call you to fulltime evangelistic ministry. Don't try to figure out how God will do it or when. But when He is ready, you will know."

In the spring of 1999, I was offered a promotion with ServiceMaster to become the Facilities Manager of Gwinnett Technical College in Lawrenceville, Georgia, in charge of custodial, grounds, and plant operations. Anything that had anything to do with building maintenance went through my departments. My bosses were, Richard Hawkshead, at the college and for ServiceMaster, Dave Robey. These guys were great to work for.

Melissa would go to the College of Charleston in Charleston, S.C.; Joseph, a junior in high school, would attend Dacula High; and Benjamin would attend Dacula Middle School. Terri took employment with the non-profit organization, Child Abuse Prevention Alliance working with families on public assistance. This was very similar to what she did in South Carolina.

This move was especially challenging for Joseph, who had made many friends at Liberty High School in Liberty. He was on the wrestling and baseball teams. He was an exceptional student and did not appreciate his life being interrupted like this. One day, he came to me about this very upset.

I said, "Joseph, I have to believe that in moving to Lawrenceville, Georgia, the Lord also has you in mind. For some reason, I believe this move will make things even better for you. Can you put a little trust in the Lord? Let's pray together and give the burden to Him."

I could tell when Joseph and I prayed it lifted a big burden from him. Joseph went on to play baseball, wrestle, and play tennis for Dacula High School in Georgia. One year, he was sixth in the state-wrestling tournament. He received thirteen hours of college credit before graduating from high school. I believe he had all "A's" with one "B" all through high school. Joseph was later accepted to the Citadel and received a full academic scholarship that paid for his whole college career. The Citadel is a very prestigious military college; some call it the West Point of the South.

Terri, the children, and I found a wonderful church called, Hebron Baptist Church in Dacula, Georgia. Our first worship service, the music was beautiful and the pastor gave a great message on the Jewish Roots of the Faith. This was confirming to me that we were in a good place and this was to be our church home. We all seemed to feel the same way. After the service, I went to say *hello* to the pastor, Larry Wynn. He was a very warm, people-oriented person. I told him of my appreciation of his message on the Jewish Roots of the Faith and that it made me feel very much at home. He asked if he could come and visit with me at my home, and we set up a time.

During our time together, I mentioned my ministry using baseball. I told him my love for Israel and a potential baseball ministry there. He told me of his love for the Jewish people and that he had been to Israel and his love for that place. Larry told me that he felt that I was sincere in my faith and that Hebron would help to provide me with resources to be a blessing to the Jewish people and worldwide baseball ministry.

Terri and I bought a beautiful home in Lawrenceville, which was much larger than the one in Liberty. It was a three-level home with white vinyl siding and a brick front, and four bedrooms upstairs. We now had plenty of room for our immediate family and plenty of room for guests. We also had a basement that we would later finish to host visiting ministry partners and family as well as include an office.

My salary continued to increase with this promotion. I continued to work with the Doyle School of Baseball and Terri was receiving a good income from her new job as well. This was a far cry from our time in Chapel Hill, N.C. We were very grateful for the Lord's goodness and our family agreed we wanted to help other people in our community, nation, and worldwide. The Lord had bestowed His goodness on this man who didn't deserve it. Even more important our children were prospering in school and in their faith in Christ.

At our new church, Pastor Wynn introduced me to one of the associate pastors, Duke Forster. Duke was a great guy and was interested in going with me to do baseball clinics in Israel. Our church was a very large one with over 8,000 members. Duke explained to me that Hebron had a recreation department and they had over 150 baseball coaches and a large group of umpires.

In 2000, my friends in Israel and I invited the Cyprus Youth National Baseball Team, ages fourteen to sixteen, to participate at Baptist Village and Kibbutz Gezer in a week long Friendship Baseball Tournament. In the mornings we would have an instructional time for players from Cyprus and Israel. We also held coach and umpire clinics in the morning and games in the afternoons. Leon Klarfeld, the president of the Israel Association, invited me to bring a team of coaches and umpires to assist them with this event.

Duke Forster helped me put together a team of coaches and umpires. Marty Clary, the former Atlanta Braves pitcher, also volunteered to help me, as he wanted to teach throwing and pitching. One of the highlights of the trip was that I got to bring my son Benjamin along. Two of his cousins played for the country of Israel. Benjamin was about thirteen at the time and we were told that the Cyprus team was thin on pitching. The Israel team agreed that if the Cyprus team ran out of pitchers, Benjamin could play for them. It came to pass that in one of the games the Cyprus team ran low on pitching and Ben got his chance. We were staying at my cousin, Billy Weisel's, home in Jerusalem and Ben was now facing one of his sons, Akiva, representing the country of Israel. Ben struck him out and Billy and I joked that night over dinner.

"Billy," I said, "I was afraid you would kick us out of your house when Ben struck your son out."

Billy was a great guy. He grew up in Champaign, Illinois. He also went to college there at the same time as me. Sometimes for Passover, his family invited me to celebrate with them. Now, I was Billy's guest in their home in Jerusalem. One morning, Billy and I were in the kitchen and spoke on the matter of Jesus.

Billy said, "Jeff, I believe that the Messiah will come in the future."

I explained to Billy that the Messiah had already come and the Torah makes that clear in the Book of Daniel, chapter 9.

He then chuckled, "When He comes, I will ask Him if He has already been here."

Billy had a good sense of humor and we have always loved and respected each other as cousins.

In the early summer of 2000, one of my former bosses with the ServiceMaster Company, John Harrison, asked me if I would share my testimony in his church, North Georgia Bible Chapel in Dawsonville, Georgia. The time at his church went extremely well and after the service his pastor, Dale Crawshaw, asked to speak with me. Dale said that he loved my testimony and how the Lord was using me in a ministry that used baseball. Dale asked me if I would return soon and speak again. He also said that his son, Ben, pitched at a school called Lee University in Cleveland, Tennessee, and had almost signed a pro contract. He explained that Ben had a dream of using baseball to go to Cuba and minister to them.

Dale said, "Jeff, you have the baseball background and administrative skills to work with Ben to put a team together."

I asked Dale how this trip would be funded. Dale told me that his church would help to fund my trip, put baseball equipment together, and that he had a publishing company that could make baseball cards of all the guys who would go with us that would have the gospel message in Spanish on the back. I told Dale I liked his ideas and would pray about this opportunity.

During this time, I also had a friend at Gwinnett Tech whose husband was an accountant. He was helping me to put a charitable non-profit organization together so that we could raise funds to be able to have a support base that would enable me to do an even better job of working with children and others through baseball. The non-profit organization would be called Global Youth Baseball Federation, Inc.

On the following Monday, I went to work and had a meeting with my boss from ServiceMaster, Dave Robey, and my Vice President of Operations, Richard Hawkshead, at Gwinnet Technical College. We were supposed to discuss opportunities for expansion that day. We were three years into a five-year contract with the college. We had lived two years in our new home, and things were just great.

To my absolute surprise, my boss with the college said, "Jeff, what I am going to say to you and Dave today is hard because I consider you a good friend. You are only two years into your new home, and I could not have had a better manager than you. Our college is struggling with the way we receive funding. We have had a short fall of funds that come into our school from the local government. As a result we are going to have to cancel our contract early."

We were all taken by surprise and Richard seemed a bit distraught to me.

I thought about what he said for a moment and said, "Well, I am glad that you have been pleased with my performance. Perhaps I will get a new job with ServiceMaster; maybe I will be able to stay in Lawrenceville and get a job in the Atlanta area so that my children do not have to move again. Perhaps the Lord wants me in full-time ministry. Now, let's get some lunch; I'm hungry."

Richard was astonished with the peace that I had at such a critical moment.

I told him that this was the peace that only the Lord can provide and I realized the Lord had a plan for my life. Then I was told I would have three months left before I would have to leave Gwinnet Tech.

A few days later, Dale Crawshaw, called me at home in the evening and said, "Are you still interested in going to Cuba?"

I said, "Yes, but I need to tell you want happened to me at my job at ServiceMaster."

When I filled Dale in on what happened, he replied, "Jeff, when I first met you I said to myself, why is Jeff not in full time ministry? I have an idea for your consideration. Why don't you ask about twenty friends to come to our church for prayer and let's seek the Lord's counsel as to His will for your life? Perhaps the Lord is getting ready to launch you into full-time ministry."

I invited about twenty friends, all from different churches and different vocations. Everyone introduced themselves and we began to pray. Then, came godly counsel. The essence of what came forward was the Lord was getting ready to call me into full-time ministry. He would show me the way and the perfect moment to begin. I had no realization at the time, but my twenty closest friends and Dale Crawshaw would become our first Board of Directors. It was not long after this meeting that I received from the IRS my non-profit 501c3 approval for Global Youth Baseball Federation, Inc.

For God is not a God of disorder but of peace.
(1 Corinthians 14:33 NIV)

Chapter 17:

Get Out of the Boat

Dale Crawshaw and I spoke about the development of Global Youth Baseball Federation, Inc. Dale had been praying about his involvement and told me that the Lord had encouraged him to give a year of his life to Global Baseball. Here is what was incredible about this commitment. Dale had a rare kidney disease and each day his kidneys continued to deteriorate. He had less than twenty percent of his function in both kidneys. It was just a matter of time that he would have to go on dialysis. His only chance for survival was to get a kidney transplant. This transplant would have to be close to an exact match or it would be rejected. Dale's helping to get Global Baseball off the ground was very humbling for me.

The Lord was providing me with Dale's selfless example. I knew that this could be the last project in his life. He told me that he believed that the Lord would provide for him a new kidney since he only needed one good one. Dale began to get sicker and sicker, and he was very close to going on dialysis. Then his daughter tested a perfect match to be a donor. Dale got his new kidney (which he calls "Isaac") and is doing much better. Dale's advice to Global Baseball had been the catalyst and a good foundation for our organization.

ServiceMaster sent me to interview at a hospital in Boca Raton, Florida, and also at the University of Mississippi at Oxford, Mississippi. They told

Dale was one of those few angels that visit us in our lifetime to bring us closer to Jesus and point the way forward.

me that I could have either of these locations. At Boca Raton, I would be offered $63,000 and in three months I would be automatically increased to $65,000. I was forty-five years old and did not want to move again for Benjamin's sake. I remember how hard it was on Joseph and this time I did not feel that we were supposed to move.

Two days before I was to leave my job at Gwinnet Tech, I came home for lunch, as my house was only ten minutes away. Over lunch this thought penetrated my mind: *Jeff, don't you see the handwriting on the wall?* I moved away from the kitchen table and knelt to pray before my couch in the living room. I was thinking to myself, *Is this the Lord speaking to me?*

The next thing I knew I was in prayer saying, "Lord, I see the writing on the wall, but I do not see the financial provision."

The Lord had me read Matthew 14:22-33. This is the story about Jesus sending His disciples into a storm in a boat. In the middle of the night, Jesus came walking on the water and told His disciples to not be afraid. Peter, who is at the edge of the boat, recognized Jesus' voice and said, "Lord, if it is You, command me to get out of the boat." Jesus said, "Come!"

I asked the Lord, "Are You saying that You are calling me to a full-time, faith-based ministry?"

I heard, "Jeff, if you want to see the financial provision you will need to leave your job and

As I continued in prayer, the Lord gave me two choices. One, I could continue in secular work and be blessed there, or come and work for Him in faith-based ministry.

attend to the development of Global Baseball."

"Lord, where do I start? When do I step away from my job at ServiceMaster?"

James 1:5-8 came to mind, and I realized that the Lord would give me the wisdom as I prayed. It would come one day at a time; I would have to be obedient one day at a time and one person at a time. This is how I would be directed as the president of Global Youth Baseball Federation, Inc.

Even as I realized the magnitude of what God was moving me into, I reminded Him, "Father, I do not feel that I have been a very good husband or father. I have made a lot of mistakes in my life."

The Lord made it clear to me, if I would be obedient to Him that He would heal the memories of the past, and I would be remembered as a godly man in the future.

"Lord, You paid the price for me 2000 years ago, and I will follow You the rest of my days in whatever You ask me to do."

When I told Terri how the Lord was directing me, she was a little afraid of me stepping out in faith. Confident this was the Lord's doing, we agreed that if we went behind on one bill I would seek new employment. Then I called Dale and the Board of Directors for Global Baseball concerning my decision to go full time. I continued to do some consulting work for ServiceMaster until Christmas break of 2000. We also took a team of fourteen guys to Cuba with the full blessing of the United States Treasury Department who gave me a two-year license to conduct religious activities in Cuba. My consulting projects with ServiceMaster ended after my return from Cuba.

Before I left for Cuba, my youngest brother, Bruce, began going to Willow Creek Church with his wife. Bruce had fallen into some personal problems and received comfort hearing testimonies from people like Mike Singletary, who played for the Chicago Bears. Before I went to Cuba, Bruce asked me how I got saved and became a completed Jew. I shared with him all the credentials of the Messiah in the Torah and my personal testimony. Bruce sat at the edge of his bed three days later and prayed with his wife to accept Jesus in his heart. His father-in-law, an associate pastor in the Church of Christ, baptized him a few months later.

If any of you lacks wisdom, let him ask of God,
who gives to all liberally and without reproach, and it will be given to him.
But let him ask in faith, with no doubting,
for he who doubts is like a wave of the sea driven and tossed by the wind.
For let not that man suppose that he will receive anything from the Lord;
he is a double minded person, unstable in all his ways. (James
1:5-8 NKJV)

Baseball program in Alamar, Cuba, for children

Jeff teaches throwing to children in Alamar, Cuba, baseball program

Jeff with children in Alamar, Cuba, after softball game

Former National Team player, Raul Valdez, and Global Baseball National Director, Pete Millar, in Latin American Stadium in Havana

George Murdock, Chairman of the Board of Directors - Global Baseball feeds children in Dominican Republic

**Brian Doyle - Yankees 1978 World Series Leading Hitter,
teaches fielding in Eilat, Israel**

Chapter 18:

Trust in the Lord with All Your Heart

Almost ready to fully get out of the boat and no longer return to ServiceMaster, I left my comfort zone and went into a ministry that would require me to raise support. Pastor Greg Sweet sent me an e-mail that ended with this Bible verse from Proverbs 3:5-6, "Trust in the Lord with all your heart, and do not rely on your own understanding; think about Him in all your ways, and He will guide you on the right paths" (HCSB). Greg always e-mails me with this reminder, and I thank the Lord for friends like Greg!

In December of 2001, we were on our way to Cuba. We traveled from Atlanta to Montego Bay, Jamaica, and then to Havana. We took Ben Crawshaw, Marty Clary, and Leon Broadleaf, who pitched at University of Illinois. We had eleven additional guys, which included me. We each had 1000 baseball cards with our pictures on the front and the plan of salvation in Spanish on the back.

Our host was Pastor Eduardo Otero. At the time, he had four little house churches and a handful of children who liked baseball in the city of Alamar, a suburb of Havana. A former pastor of Siloam Baptist Church recommended Eduardo to me as he had been to Cuba to minister in Eduardo's house churches. He told me that Eduardo had a dream of using baseball in his country to reach people for Jesus Christ. Eduardo and I connected in the Atlanta airport when he was on his way home from Louisville, Kentucky, where he had ministered for the last ten days. Eduardo and I had a very similar vision how baseball could be a blessing in his community, Havana, and eventually over the whole island of Cuba.

Eduardo had suggested a baseball tournament with eight teams participating, speaking in churches, home visitations, and baseball clinics for children. He also asked if we could donate baseball equipment so that he could start a little league program and some humanitarian aid like vitamins, toothbrushes, shoes, socks, razors, shaving cream, and blood pressure cuffs. These are all essentials you would get at Wal-Mart but are not available in Cuba.

Each of us had two seventy-pound bags, one of our clothes and one of the humanitarian aid that Eduardo requested. Upon our arrival, we could feel the presence that only communism can offer (total control). The airport was swarming with military. When we went through immigration, customs agents questioned us as to why we had so much baseball equipment and humanitarian aid.

Through miracles, we were allowed to bring in all of our things. They liked baseball and when we said that we were participating in a tournament, they asked us for a ball or two and let us go through. They even asked us for some vitamins for their families. We were now in the Havana airport parking lot and it was good to see Pastor Eduardo. We all jumped on the church bus and went to our hotel.

Our hotel stay was hilarious at times. Everything seemed to be fine until at night the power would purposely be turned off. One time I was fully lathered up in the shower and the water was turned off. I heard screams of frustration from our guys as they were all showering as well.

Our first game was incredible. Ben Crawshaw was on the mound. He was doing a great job. Marty Clary at first base, and Leon Broadleaf, also known as

Flexibility is the golden word when you travel to other countries. You go with the flow.

Smooth Broadway in college, was at second base. Going into the last inning we were leading 6-4. Marty hit two towering home runs. The Cuban team was freaking out. Not bad for a throw-together team of has-beens. We were holding our own and Eduardo was impressed. The captain of the other team, Raul Valdez, was a sure-handed third baseman who was a sleek six-foot-two and could hit for power. He had played in the Cuban Professional Leagues on a team called the Metros in Havana. He also had played on the Cuban National Team. He helped his team come back and win the game 7-6 in the top of the ninth. We had a respectable first game.

Leon Broadleaf, who pitched for the University of Illinois, in the late 1970s, was going to share his personal testimony that night in the main house church meeting. Everyone on our university team called Leon, "Smooth Broadway" or "Smooth. He was the only guy who could get away with wearing a purse on campus. Leon wore his smooth shirts and white bellbottom pants on our university campus with big mutton chop sideburns and a mustache. Leon may not have known where the classrooms were located, and I am not sure he even bought books for the classes. One day during our senior year when we played the University of Indiana, he was the starting pitcher. His fastball was in the 90s that day and the other team could not catch up with his blinding speed. He also had an incredible curve to match.

He told the other team, "I'm throwing a fastball and you can't hit it."

Our head coach was freaking out and kept popping tablets that were in a little metal pillbox. I'm not sure what they were but probably had something to do with stress relief. Leon went on to strike out eleven batters in a row; we won the game.

Friends from The Fellowship of Christian Athletes shared about Jesus with Leon. He gave his life to Christ at the end of his senior year. He really changed after coming to Christ and has led a very fulfilled life since.

Raul Valdez, captain of the opposing Cuban team, came to hear Leon that night in the main house church. Leon shared his full story on how he came to Christ in college. When an altar call was provided, Raul came forward and gave his life to Christ. Many people also came forward that night from the community.

The city of Alamar, where Pastor Eduardo established his main house church, was to have been a model communist city in the '60s and '70s. Fidel Castro had many supervisors come from the Soviet Union to live in this city and help get a firm communist grip on his nation. With his failed system in place for over fifty years, we visited this city where people were hungry to know their Maker. Raul and many others now know Fidel Castro is not their provider.

A few days later, we had another meeting at the main house church and Raul decided to come back with his wife, children, mom, and grandfather-in-law, Pedro.

His teammates from the all-star team that Pastor Eduardo put together came to his apartment and said, "Raul, what are you doing tonight?"

He said, "I'm going to church with my family."

All his teammates said, "Raul, if you are going to church, we want to go, too."

Marty Clary, who pitched with the Atlanta Braves (1987-90), spoke this time, and when he gave the altar call, the whole team came forward to confess Jesus and became Christians. It was an incredible time of baseball games and children's clinics during the day, then church meetings and baptismal services at night and on Sunday. We left Cuba seeing over one hundred people ask Jesus in their hearts. Pastor Eduardo had the additional baseball equipment to begin a little league program, and asked us to come back multiple times the next year with a larger team.

When I came home from my trip to Cuba, I called my brother Bruce to see how he was doing with the Lord and his family life. He explained that he was doing well and his family life had improved. Bruce asked me if I would explain to my father his decision to follow the Lord Jesus. I said okay, but I was thinking to myself, *Can a person get kicked out of their family two times?* I had to tell my dad that Bruce had come to the same conclusion that I had—that Jesus is the promised Jewish Messiah.

When I did, I received the surprise of my life. Instead of becoming angry as he had when I made my decision to follow Jesus, he said, "Bruce has made a good decision. I see the change in his life."

My dad was aware of Bruce's personal and family problems and had seen the improvement.

He then continued, "Jeff, will you forgive me for having rejected you many years ago? I thought you stopped being Jewish, but now I realize you are more Jewish than me. Can you explain to me from the Bible where Jesus said He is the Messiah and the Son of God?"

I was amazed, but managed to say, "Sure, Dad, I would be glad to."

> *Jesus and his disciples went out to the towns of Caesarea Philippi; and on the road he asked his disciples, saying to them, "Who do men say that I am?" So they answered, "John the Baptist, but some say Elijah and others say one of the prophets." But he said to them, "But who do you say that I am?" Peter answered Him, "You are the Christ." (Mark 8:27-29)*

Jesus answered and said to him, "Blessed are you, Simon Bar-Jonah, for flesh and blood has not revealed this to you, but my Father who is in heaven." (Matthew 16:17)

I explained to my dad that this is where Jesus was explaining to Peter that his assessment was true. Then I had the opportunity to share my testimony with my dad and the verses in the Torah and Prophets that make it certain that only Jesus could have fulfilled these Bible prophesies.

At the end of our conversation my dad said, "Well, it is all there."

"What do you mean it is all there?" I asked.

"I see it, finally," he said. "I now realize that Jesus is Messiah for the Jewish people and all mankind. Will you pray with me like you do with the children at your baseball programs?"

"Dad, are you saying that you want to invite Jesus in your heart?" I asked.

"Yes, son, that is what I am saying," then he began to cry in the Hebrew language, "*Henaini, Henaini*, Lord," (which means, "Here I am, here I am, Lord.")

He then cried out, "Lord, what would You have me to do?"

As I listened and waited, my Dad said, "Jeff, all these years someone has been calling to me and now I know who it is."

My dad began to weep, and as I prayed with him, he asked the Lord to forgive his sins, and fill him with His Holy Spirit. My dad asked for the Lord to lead him and guide him the rest of his days. From that moment on I had a new dad and a brother in Christ. Second Corinthians 5:17 says, "Therefore, if anyone is in Christ, he is a new creation; old things have passed away; behold all things have become new."

In January 2002, I had the opportunity to participate in a church conference at Midway Macedonia Baptist Church in Carrollton, Georgia. It started on a Wednesday and ended on Saturday. They asked if we could do a baseball clinic in their gymnasium. We had five guys from Global Baseball participate. About one hundred children came and parents made donations of baseball equipment to our organization. Marty Clary shared the gospel message during the baseball program and five children committed their lives to Christ. I really enjoyed this church, as they had been very kind to our organization and to me.

After this church conference, I received an incredible phone call from my mom.

She said, "Your brother Rick is on the way to your home from Chicago. It is the middle of the night! I am afraid he will harm himself driving!"

I said, "Mom, he will be okay, I promise."

After years of prayer, I knew the Lord was going to bring him safely to our home. Rick had fallen into some family and financial problems. He arrived early the next day and I put him to bed as I could see he was very tired. When he got up, he went for a walk in the neighborhood and then came into the house.

He sat down and broke down in my arms, "I am not as hard-hearted as you think."

"Why have you come to this house?' I asked him. "You could have gone to mom or Bruce. Why here?"

"There is love in this house and I know you will tell me what I need to hear, not what I want to hear."

For about three months, Terri and I loved on my brother, Rick, and encouraged him that the Lord wanted to give him a new life. He even came with me for a counseling session with our associate pastor at Hebron Baptist. Rick actually came to our church and loved to hear the messages our pastor, Larry Wynn, gave saying they were very loving and practical.

After three months, Rick decided to get his own place, found employment in the Atlanta area, and began a new life. He did not come to Jesus at that time, but he was much softer and our relationship improved as a result. I believe that in God's time, the Lord will reveal Himself to Rick as he did to my dad and our brother, Bruce.

In May of 2002, I received a phone call from a member of Midway Macedonia Baptist Church, Rob Robinson. He told me that the baseball clinic was one of highlights of the conference and that they had a trip planned to Brazil. He told me that a man had built a baseball stadium on the Paraguay River in the city of Corumba. He said that they had a few kids to train and that more were signing up. They needed me to go and take the lead role. I asked how many children had signed up and he said over three hundred.

"Wow," I said, "we could start a church with these kids and families."

I told them that we would need to invest about $3500 in baseball gloves, balls, and collect used bats, helmets, catcher gear, etc. A few days later, Mr. Robinson said that they had raised the money and would pay for my trip. When we went we had about fifteen bags of baseball equipment and had over three hundred and twenty-five children in attendance. We saw about two hundred and ten children give their lives to Jesus after the baseball program and fourteen parents accepted Christ after watching the Jesus film in Portuguese.

When the trip came to an end, Pastor Carl King, who lived in Corumba with his family, took me to a small mountain overlooking the field. It had a large statue of Christ that looked like the one in Rio de Janeiro. He asked me if I had any idea who built this stadium. I told him I had no idea. He explained to me, He and friends of the Baptist Pantanal Project thought that baseball could be used as a platform to help children come to Christ, learn Christian values, and have a better life. They thought this baseball stadium, and others that would be developed later, could also help children and families become connected to local churches in Corumba and neighboring cities.

Carl explained to me that he, and those involved with the Pantanal Project, were praying for a supervisor for the project and they felt it should be me. He asked me to pray about how we could place an American, who had some background in baseball, full time in Corumba. I accepted the challenge, and we put, Sonny Miller, from Villa Rica, Georgia, in a full-time position there. He came and worked with the children from 2003-2008.

Sonny was a very courageous young man in that he did not know the language and the setting was very rural. He quickly learned the language and worked with the children and pastors of the city of Corumba and Ladario. On Sonny's first trip to Corumba, he met a Brazilian dentist who was a volunteer on one of the mission trips led by Carl King. Carl had a beautiful medical boat built for this ministry along the Paraguay River. Sonny and the dentist, Karina, fell in love and were married after a lovely courtship.

When we would bring American teams, we invited the mayor to come and throw out the first ball. During our time in Corumba, a local television station did a documentary about our work through baseball with the children of the city. The television documentary was shown in multiple Brazilian cities, one of which was Campo Grande, about six hours away by car.

Now Brazil has the second largest population of Japanese people in the world. Sao Paulo has over one million Japanese people. Campo Grande has the second largest population of Japanese in Brazil. The Brazil National Baseball Team is comprised of mostly Japanese players. We received a phone call from the Japanese Baseball Federation Association Campo Grande Baseball (ACB). They told us that they had seen the documentary and desired to play us in our stadium in Corumba. They came in the summer of 2003 with a team of ten to twelve year olds and an older team of twelve and older. Their younger children beat us comfortably, but our older children tied their older team.

The Japanese coaches were impressed that in two years we could play their children competitively. That evening we had dinner together and I asked them if they minded if I did devotion for their children on Sunday morning before our games. They said no problem and we had a great devotional time. Japanese parents and coaches came and thanked me for taking this time to teach their children Christian values.

The next day, our older children won their game by one run and it was like winning the World Series. This was also the beginning of a long-term friendship with the Japanese Baseball Federations in Brazil. Baptist pastors in Corumba and Campo Grande said that the Japanese were a closed people group and hard to reach for Jesus. Baseball became a common denominator for us and we developed lasting friendships.

Our new friends invited us to Campo Grande in 2004-2006. We saw many come to Christ by bringing Christian baseball teams, karate teams, and softball teams. At one karate demonstration, we saw forty-five Japanese people living in Campo Grande confess Christ, and they were not all children. The president of the Campo Grande Japanese Baseball Federation was seventy years old and gave his life to Jesus.

On one occasion, we were invited by the Japanese Federation to the city of Navarai. There were also multiple Japanese Federations from various cities competing in softball. I was even asked to play shortstop for the Japanese Softball Federation of Campo Grande. During a special evening dinner I was introduced to some of the presidents of the federations in various cities.

We had brought a FCA team of fifteen to seventeen year olds from Centreville, Virginia. George Murdock, a friend of mine and chairman of the Board of Directors for Global Baseball, brought his team. They played in a baseball tournament and made donations of baseball equipment to the Baseball Federation in Navarai.

The presidents of the federations of other cities in Brazil said, "Please bring your teams to our cities. Our children are having problems with drugs and teen sex. Please teach our children the Bible and baseball."

When the Japanese invite us they always offer us hotel lodging for our teams and meals, and even an invitation to stay in their homes in the future. What gracious hosts!

One of our success stories in Brazil is about a young man named Ravel. He came to our baseball training sessions in Corumba, Brazil. He was about thirteen years old in 2003. When he was five, he was in the kitchen having some breakfast. In his parents' bedroom his father killed his mother and then left the home. Ravel had to move in with his grandmother. His father was later killed so this young boy grew up without a mother or a father. Ravel began to attend our baseball programs and found the Lord Jesus Christ through the ministry of baseball in Corumba. He began to go to church at the Pantanal Project headquarters. After a few years of mentoring, Ravel was baptized. When Ravel became twenty years old, he married and they had a baby. He became our field director when Sonny and Karina left to go to America, and was on a full time salary and worked on completing high school.

Kids like Ravel would be running the street, in jail, in gangs, on drugs or involved in other criminal activities. Now

Has the baseball ministry made a difference? You bet!

these same kind of kids are learning to run the bases, instead of running the streets. Because of his changed life in Christ, Ravel was looked up to by all the kids in the baseball project who joined him in going to church. They said, "If Ravel can make it so can we."

In 2001, when we began in Cuba, Pastor Eduardo had four house churches and a handful of children. By 2003, we began to bring churches and the Lee University baseball program multiple times. Pastor Eduardo and his congregants looked forward to our coming each time as they now had twenty-eight house churches. While doing ministry with one of our groups in Cuba, Raul Valdez, the national baseball player, asked me if we would like to come as his guest to a pro game at the Latin American Stadium. You didn't have to bend any of our arms on that one. During the game, Raul introduced me to the son of a key government official. I am not at liberty to tell you who this is, but this person helped us get to places we needed to go and later gave his life to Jesus. The sons of the Revolution are now becoming Christians and opening their homes for Bible studies.

Cuba is a special place. The Holy Spirit is sweeping this nation through the house church movement and many are receiving Christ and are being discipled. We have been doing home visits, pastoral training in doctrine and evangelism, and have been bringing musicians and humanitarian aid.

In 2010, I met with a government official who is the only one who can grant ships access to the Havana harbor. He asked me many questions that are typical of a communist official. I turned to him and said, "Do you really want to know everything about Global Baseball?" He said, "Yes." I remarked, "Kids running the streets or running the bases, it's up to you and me." I said, "I am not a political person but I do love the people of Cuba and your children. Can we partner together to reach the children before they get in trouble? We can use baseball to teach them discipline and self-esteem. The children are the future of the nations." This official smiled and said, "You will always be welcome here and any items that you want to send to help the church and the children of Cuba will be approved and be sent wherever you ask." I was in shock and found this man and other officials to be honorable. I am able to do things in Cuba that I never would have thought possible. This as well can only be the Lord's doing.

As of the year 2015, we now have eighty house churches and many government officials have given their lives to Jesus. We have been granted religious visas from the Director of Religious Affairs for anyone who comes with Global Baseball to Cuba. We now have a three-building complex that has been remodeled with the ability to house up to sixty people. It has hot showers, air conditioning, and a new kitchen. We no longer have to stay in broken down government hotels and the funds will now stay with the church to provide jobs for their people.

In 2013, a lady across the street from the main church asked me to purchase her home for the church. She said that she appreciated the work we were doing for children and families. To purchase her home I would need to obtain permission from the US and Cuban governments. Both were miraculously granted and also funds were raised beyond my ability to do so. This could only be the hand of the Lord.

Many have given their lives to the Lord through home visits and evangelism programs. People are getting saved in their homes and apartments and offering them for Bible studies and house churches. I am bringing pastors and theological professors to do a more formal house church seminary so that the house church leaders will be able to teach proper doctrine and theology and lead their congregants in a more effective way.

The Cuban government has granted us permission to go anywhere on the island to share Jesus and plant churches. They have asked us to help people who do not know Jesus with humanitarian aid and to put new roofs on homes that have been damaged by hurricanes. We desire to help the leaders come to the place where we are no longer needed and they can take their nation forward to reach the lost for Christ and make disciples.

In 2002, my dad and I were invited by my friend, Neal Siegel, to Elkhorn, Wisconsin, to his cottage on a beautiful lake. The purpose of our visit was a men's Bible retreat. My dad was very excited to get to know Christian men in his own age group. We had devotions on various subjects and the time was sweet.

One day after our devotion time, we all decided to go out back to the lake and go jet skiing and pontoon boating. As I and the other men were getting close to where the boats were docked, my dad was lagging a distance behind. We heard him shout to us!

"Guys, you are forgetting something."

I said, "Dad, what are we forgetting?"

He said, "I need to be baptized."

I was pleasantly surprised. He asked Neal to baptize him in the lake with me on his right hand. He came out of the water a new man in Christ. There was an incredible change from that day on. He is one who knows what it means from his heart for a Jewish person to be water baptized.

During the early summer of 2003, I was invited to share my personal testimony on a Christian television station, LaSea Broadcasting in South Bend, Indiana. They invited me to share my personal testimony on their Harvest show. When I got done, I visited my dad in Downers Grove, Illinois, and he drove with me to our home in Lawrenceville, Georgia. We had about three great weeks together with Terri and our children. During my dad's time in our home, my mom's husband, Jack Cohen got sick with stroke-like symptoms and was in the hospital. My mom was very distraught. I told my dad about this situation.

To my surprise, Dad asked to speak with my mom the next time I called her.

He said, "Shirley, I feel your pain for Jack."

My dad had hated Jack Cohen, feeling like he interfered with his marriage when he was married to my mom. But now he had forgiven this man and asked my mom if he could pray for him.

My mom said, "Please pray for him."

To my surprise my dad said, "Shirley, when I pray for Jack, the Lord is going to heal him."

He explained to her that Jesus is the Lord and if you leave Jesus out of the picture you leave God out as well. He prayed in the name of Jesus and Jack was well in less than two weeks. After I sent my dad home on the plane back to Chicago, Illinois, my mom recognized the change in my dad's life, and they fully reconciled and became friends.

A few weeks later, I was doing some work at home with my friends remodeling our basement when I received a call from my brother, Bruce. It was August 16, 2003. He said that my dad had died of a heart attack in his apartment. He was sixty-nine years old and not in the best of health. I honestly was not ready for him to leave. I was enjoying my times with my dad who was a fellow believer in Jesus and now he was gone. After I told my friends who were helping me sheet rock the basement, I broke down and cried. It felt the strangest for me in the evenings when I would in times past have called my dad, but now he was not there to call anymore. I miss him a lot.

My brothers asked me to do the funeral. My mom found out about this and asked me to not speak about Jesus. I expressed my respect for her, but also told her I would have to honor my dad's wishes. I knew he would want me to speak about his faith in Jesus at his funeral. She called my brother Rick and asked him to stop me from talking about Jesus, and he told her that I would speak what would be appropriate for the occasion.

At the funeral my brothers, Rick and Bruce, went first and talked about their lives with our dad. I did a lot of the same and transitioned to how important it was to my dad to send us to Hebrew School to receive Bar Mitzvah training and to understand what it meant to be a Jew. My dad loved going to the Sabbath or High Holiday services, and enjoyed listening to Rabbi Gold's sermons. I then explained to the audience that in my dad's last years he met the most famous Rabbi that ever lived. I told them that he loved to listen to this Rabbi's sermons even more than Rabbi Gold's. I then explained to the audience the credentials of this Rabbi and explained to them He was the Jewish Messiah (Yeshua-Jesus).

You could hear a pin drop in the room. All eyes were glued on me and no one was angry except my mom. My brother, Rick, came to me and fell at my feet and kissed my hands. It was a very emotional time for him. Later at the funeral, my dad's friends, Phillip and Laura Schlesinger (Uncle Boo-boo and Aunt Laurie) told me about an interaction they had with my dad about two weeks before he died. They told me that he told them how he made peace with God through Jesus. They said that the change in his life was apparent and that they longed for the same peace he had. My dad planted a seed!

In 2006, I had the opportunity to speak in a church outside Richmond, Virginia. I was participating as a member of the Federation of Baptist World Ministries at the Learning Center for the International Mission Board at our yearly meeting. One of the church members who heard me speak came to see me when I was having lunch, and gave me a copy of Franklin Graham's book, *Rebel with a Cause*. In his book, it spoke about Franklin becoming a pilot and using humanitarian aid to earn the right to speak with people about Jesus. Out of this compassion for people, Franklin sent aid wherever it was needed and it helped people to see God's love in a tangible way.

One day, after reading this book on a trip to Brazil, I felt the Lord speak to me and say that I should go and get my pilot's license. In the future, I would put a group of doctors and pilots together and bring humanitarian aid to different parts of the world. I had even talked to, Pastor Carl King, about it at the time.

I began my pilot training at the Gwinnett County airport about two miles from our home in the spring of 2006. Twenty hours into my training, I went for my flight physical as one could not solo until you took this physical. When I was filling out the documents for the physical, it asks if you have ever committed a crime or a felony. Yes, I had. I thought that the Lord had spoken to me but it looked like this might be an issue with me obtaining my license.

I immediately spoke with the doctor, who was with the FAA, and was honest about my past and also the present. He began to say that one who has committed a felony couldn't be a pilot. Then he put his arm around me and said, in certain cases under FAA guidelines this could be forgiven and put in the past. He said that he was going to recommend me for what was called "an exception."

I said, "Doc, how could you recommend me having been with me for less than an hour?"

He said that the man standing before him was not the same person who committed the crime, "Please write your testimony for me in a Microsoft Word document and also send me your brochures and accomplishments of Global Baseball. Then also send the testimony of raising your children."

I asked the doctor if I should stop taking lessons until the FAA ruled on my situation. He told me there was no reason to stop and that I should go forward. He told me I would hear from them in few weeks to a month.

As I was walking out the doctor said, "Don't worry, you will also be a good pilot."

I was in shock. What just happened? I got in my car and had to pick up a few things on the way home for Terri at Sam's Club.

When I found a parking space in a quiet spot, I broke down and cried, "Lord, is there something you are after? I thought I heard Your voice! What is it that You want?"

He said, **"I want you to write a book about your life and about hope! Tell those where I send you about the great things I have done for you.** When you turned to Me, I turned to you and have watched over you all these years, and I have never let you down."

I said, "Lord, if You will put in the FAA's heart to approve me so I can go on to get my private pilot's license, then You will get the book."

Two weeks later, I got a letter in the mail from the FAA saying that I have been approved by them and to go ahead and get my private pilot's license. Less than a year later, I was tested and passed on the first try. What a miracle!

October 27, 2006, I had the opportunity to speak on WBPI TV Channel 49 in North Augusta, S.C. The owner of the station, Dorothy Spaulding, invited me to share my testimony on her Christian television show at 9:00 p.m. It was a great night. Terri was with me and praying in the audience. During the breaks, an African-American evangelist sang and had a beautiful voice. After the show, he came to me and gave me a word from the Lord.

He said, "In the days ahead, the Lord will open up the door to a new house. When this comes to pass all the treasure that the Lord has put in your life will be able to come out."

At the time of this man's speaking to me, I was enjoying being a part of Hebron Baptist Church and had been there about eight years. We had a great pastor, mission pastor, and staff. I loved the people of Hebron and we visited and ministered in Israel, Cuba, Brazil, and the Dominican Republic together. I couldn't have been happier.

This evangelist also told me that there was a ministry that the Lord had for me that I had not been comfortable with and had pushed the idea away for many years. He told me that a day was coming when I would wake up and flow in this ministry. The Lord would take away the discomfort. I began to pray and search how I was going to make the transition to Jewish ministry as my burden for my kinsmen had been growing. I realized I needed additional schooling and cultural training in order to minister to Jewish people.

When I was involved with the church in Spokane, I was in a pastoral leadership position and I had failed. I was too young, did not possess the appropriate character to be in this position, and was not properly trained. I had convinced myself as a result of my failure this was never to be my calling and that I had sinned too badly to revisit this in my life. I am an evangelist and very content and happy to be a soul winner for Christ. My thoughts were, *Lord, please do not call upon me to be a pastor or to work in that sphere, as I do not have the ability. I do not see this as something I desire or that You could ever desire for me.*

A few years earlier in 2004, my friend, Bob Alexander, had approached his pastor, Don Dunavant, at Siloam Baptist Church and asked him what he thought about ordaining me. Don thought this was a great idea. Since I was now a member of Hebron, he was of the opinion that it would be best for me to do this at my new home congregation. Since I was so busy with the baseball ministry I did not pursue this. It was not important to me at the time.

In 2006, a pastor from Brazil, Gilson Breder, stayed in our home for four months learning English. We spent a lot of time together traveling and ministering in American and Brazilian churches. We became very close. He is the pastor of First Baptist Church in Campo Grande, Mato Grosso do Sul, Brazil. We developed some large projects together with his church, which had over 5,000 very committed believers. He allowed me to speak in his pulpit, to share my testimony and to teach the Word of God.

Every Monday morning from 9:00 a.m. until noon, many of the pastors from the city of Campo Grande play indoor soccer as a stress reliever and a source of fellowship. When I was in town, I was always invited and had a lot of fun with these guys. Sometimes I was invited to speak in additional churches through this network. In addition, Gilson would invite me to stay in his home and I was accepted as part of his family. He would take me to minister to families and out with friends to dinner engagements as well.

Gilson commented one day, "Jeff, all the pastors of the city of Campo Grande accept you as a fellow pastor. Why don't you go to your mission pastor and ask about the ordination process? Why don't you get ordained as it will be helpful in your future ministry?"

I did this, and my mission pastor connected me with our mentoring pastor. I received mentoring at Hebron for about two years. I was licensed by Hebron Baptist Church and ordained in March of 2008. The Lord is good but I did not see myself pastoring in a local congregational setting. One thing I began to recognize was that out of the brokenness of my past, local pastors trusted me with their lives as one who was a source of encouragement.

I had become a gentler person, who could identify with pastors' lonely moments, and understand the challenges in their ministries and lives.

In 2006, I received a call from Vic Jacobson, the president of Hope Now, which had a ministry to orphans in the Ukraine. He said that he had looked at the web site of Global Baseball and wanted to invite my wife and me to the city of Cherkassy, Ukraine, and see their ministry to orphans. Terri and I agreed to go and realized that we would land in the capitol city of Kiev. Kiev is where my grandfather, Joseph Nemerow, was born.

May 11-25, 2007, Terri and I went to the cities of Cherkassy and Kiev in the Ukraine. While working in Cherkassy, our interpreter, a young man named Dima, said we were invited to the campgrounds of one of the largest Messianic congregations in the world. It is called the Kiev Messianic Jewish Congregation. They told Dima that they had heard about Jeff Siegel and how he ministered to children through sports.

The campground was a large piece of land that had been a former Soviet camp. It needed some work, but it was a good place for the congregation to meet for special times. One morning, I went with Dima to the outside shower. The huge tank of water, supported high in the air, was supposed to be heated by the sun. I got a little water on me and began to lather up. Instead of getting warmer the water became as cold as ice. I had to get the soap off and knew that I was going to have to get under the cold water.

As I rinsed off with the freezing water, I screamed in a Russian accent, "Strong like bull!"

Dima couldn't stop laughing. A few hundred feet away, Terri could hear us and began to laugh as well. Dima went for some groceries and made some eggs for Terri and me with something that looked like salami in it. The meat was very red and very tasty.

I asked Dima, "What is that delicious meat that you put in the eggs?"

He said it was sausage made from horsemeat. Next time I won't ask! We stayed at the campsite for a few nights and I was invited by their leadership to share my personal testimony at their young people's service.

After sharing my testimony, I gave the microphone to the worship leader and she said, "Brother Jeff, you need to give an altar call."

So I did, and to my surprise the whole congregation came forward, many of them Jews. They either came to ask Jesus into their heart, to rededicate their lives, or to ask for prayer. I never saw so many Jewish people come forward at once anywhere else in the world. Over one hundred people came forward. They also told me that they planted and support a congregation in St. Petersburg, Russia, and that in the future they desire for me to come and minister there as well.

Trust in the Lord with all your heart, and do not rely
on your own understanding; think about Him in all your ways,
and He will guide you on the right paths.
(Proverbs 3:5-6 HCSB)

Chapter 19:

Go Back to Your People

At this time, my friend and mentor, Toby Kahr, began to encourage me that a day was coming when the worldwide baseball ministry would be absorbed as a part of a greater whole. He explained that the Lord would transition me first to the Jewish people and then to minister among the nations.

As Terri and I began to pray, we felt we would be moving to New York and would begin ministering among the Jewish people. We knew we would need wisdom on how to proceed.

While we knew we were to minister among the Jewish people, we first wondered if we would go to Israel. For that I would need some additional study in the Hebrew language and Christian theology and doctrine. A program opened up to take a Masters of Divinity in Jewish Studies at a satellite program in Manhattan, N.Y. through Biola University and Talbot Theological Seminary. Two thirds of the program would be on the Manhattan campus and for three summers I would need to go La Mirada campus in California. I finished this program in Jewish studies in May of 2012, which gave me the tools to be a more effective minister among my Jewish brethren.

In June of 2008, Terri and I began our Abrahamic journey to New York in obedience to the Lord to establish a worldwide headquarters for Global Youth Baseball Federation, Inc. Terri and I knew we were to transition to New York and we would have to take it one day at a time, letting the Lord take care of the details.

Then miracles, one after another after another, began to unfold. The Lord is so good!

In conversation, one of our supporters said, "You are moving your ministry to New York to minister to the Jewish community at a time when our economy is experiencing a downturn. It will cost you twice as much to live there. How can you do this at this time?"

I explained, "I received this calling from the Lord Himself. I trust the matter to Him. The Lord does not want me to worry about how the practical workings will fall into place. If I take care of His business, He will take care of mine. His business is human beings. As God has been faithful to me as I have moved among the nations, He will also be faithful to me when I move among His chosen people. Where the Lord resides, there is no economic downturn."

The Lord said to Abram, "Get out of your country, from your family and from your father's house, to a land that I will show you...I will bless those who bless you, and I will curse him who curses you" (Genesis 12:1, 3 NKJV). In 2001, when the Lord called me to faith-based ministry, Terri had full-time employment and we did not have to move our home. The Lord told me that for me to see the provision I had to get out of the boat as Peter did in the Bible. Now we were ready to go on a more Abraham-like journey together to New York and Terri had to get out of the boat as well. As she said yes to the Lord, within a few weeks a miracle happened for her. The Nordstrom Company where she worked announced that they were going to open a new Nordstrom Rack store in White Plains, N.Y. This was all the confirmation she needed. In May, she put in for a transfer with Nordstrom. I also was led to a Christian realtor who specialized in rental property who helped us rent our home in Georgia. In late June, Terri was given one week to relocate to New York.

Around 2006, a Sunday school class at Hebron Baptist Church volunteered to help stuff over 1200 of my newsletters with envelopes every other month. During all this time they had followed the ministry of Global Baseball and our transition to New York. I asked the class in March to pray with us about our decision to move.

During the month of May, a lady in the class came up to me and said that the Lord had put in her and her husband's hearts to help us with our move. She invited our son, Benjamin, to live in their home while he attended graduate school at UGA. She said that she also realized that any home we would live in would be smaller than our six-bedroom home in Lawrenceville. She invited us to their home the following Tuesday evening.

We pulled up to the brand-new, huge home of Grace and John Wasczek in Bethlehem, Georgia. Grace took us around the 5500 square foot home on two acres of land with an in-ground swimming pool in the backyard. Grace took us upstairs to the room she was proposing for Benjamin, very large and beautiful. Then she took us downstairs and showed Terri and me our quarters when we would visit Ben. She showed us other rooms for Joseph and Melissa when we would all come in on the holidays.

Terri and I were in shock as I said, "Grace, are you sure that this is what you and John want to do?" Grace said that she realized that we would need to store some of our belongings in Georgia, as we would temporarily downsize while living in smaller quarters. Grace and John had room downstairs in their basement that was large enough to store our furniture temporarily without creating an inconvenience.

Grace and John then began to tell us of the miracle of how they obtained this home, and it was their pleasure to help us with the belief that this was the Lord's will. On the way out, after Grace had given us some good southern sweet tea, Terri and I realized that the grace of God had gone before us from Bethlehem to help us in our move to New York.

The Lord was beginning to answer prayers that we hadn't even prayed yet. What a good God and Father.

As reality set in and Terri was now in White Plains, I had to move the remainder of our belongings to Grace's home before July 15, the time our new renters would arrive in our home in Lawrenceville, Georgia. We decided to rent our home in Lawrenceville and not to sell it at that time due to an economic slowdown. We would build up equity in our home until the economy would improve.

On June 24, I decided to go the Atlanta Braves evening game for a little stress relief with a few of my friends. On the way to the game, a man overlooked traffic as he was pulling away from a stop sign and hit my front end. What a terrible time for this to happen to me. Terri was in New York with our Jeep Cherokee, and I was going to the Dominican Republic on June 30. I got out of the van to see if this man and his wife were okay. He was an older African-American gentleman, Carrolton Smith, in his seventies. I asked him if he was okay, and he seemed a little disoriented. He explained to me that he had just received chemotherapy for pancreatic cancer and felt hopeless.

I asked Mr. Smith if he knew Jesus as his Lord and Savior and he said, *yes,* and that he was born again, but was having a tough time. I asked the policeman if he was a Christian and he also said yes. I told him that I needed to pray for the man involved in the accident with me. As I began to pray, Mr. Smith began to weep. I explained to him that we are not a people without hope, that the Lord could heal him or even extend time to him. However, if he died knowing Jesus, he would receive a healing beyond his imagination. His wife concurred saying that this was her word to him as well.

The van was still drivable and I went to the Braves game with my friends and had a good time. On June 30, the GEICO Insurance company called me and told me that they had totaled my van because the cost of fixing it was beyond its worth. I was in the Miami airport on my way to the Dominican Republic. What was I going to do? I called my friend, Neal Siegel, in Chicago and asked him to pray with me, and also my friend, John Van Brunt, in Lawrenceville, Georgia.

When I returned from the Dominican Republic, GEICO offered me $1,758.00. I accepted as I felt that they had tried to be fair. I also realized that this happened in the Lord's sovereign will and He had a reason. As I prayed, I remembered a friend who was a Christian lawyer in Athens, Georgia. Years ago he went with me to minister in Cuba. He helped me when my car broke down to obtain a rental for a ten-day ministry speaking tour with Pastor Eduardo. He asked a friend who owns Akins Ford in Winder, Georgia, if he could help me. I also called Marshal Britt who also works at Akins Ford and goes to my home church. He told me to call the next day and he would check to see if there was a car they could let me have for a good price.

When I called the next day, Marshal said that they found a Ford Taurus 2003 in mint condition, low mileage. When I went to meet Marshal, he pointed the car out to me and it looked brand new. We went for a test drive and I knew this was the car. Marshal introduced me to Jimmy, the salesman who would do the paperwork. I asked the cost of the car. He said that it would be $4,900.00 including everything. They explained that they were not making anything on this car and took all the profit out for me. What a miracle from the Lord! Does the Lord know where we live? I think so!

At Akin Ford at 8:00 a.m. in the morning, the workforce begins with devotions and prayer. Jimmy, Marshal, Brad Akin, and others are fine people. Upon finishing the sale of the car, Jimmy brought Brad Akin to see me. Brad remembered me from years ago. He is a very friendly kind-hearted person who has helped many people. Next door is the YMCA that Mr. Akin helped get started. Mr. Akin asked me how the ministry was going and about my son, Benjamin, who was going to the University of Georgia in the fall. I explained to him about our move to New York and that Benjamin was going to live with some friends about fifteen minutes from the Ford dealership.

Brad said he wanted me to bring Benjamin to meet him before we left, as he desired to help him if he needed anything while Terri and I were away. This was an incredible gesture. Jimmy, the salesman offered to follow me in the new car. When he dropped me off at home he asked me if we had any additional prayer requests. I asked him if he would pray for housing in New York during devotion time at work. Not the usual way a car salesman closes a deal!

On July 19, 2008, Terri went to look for housing in the Westchester County area. She found a very nice attic apartment in the home of an architect. It was 1200 square feet, with a separate entrance, parking and within walking distance of her job and the train station that would take me to Manhattan.

While moving our furniture from our home to Grace and John's, John Van Brunt, gave me some words of encouragement and wisdom. We stopped at a Checkers hamburger place to get a sandwich before closing time. We were sitting outside at a table where there were other empty tables. John pointed at two of them in proximity of ours.

"These are the tables of life," he said. "Like seasons in our life, they serve to prepare us for the next table."

He explained to me that my work with the Doyle School and the ServiceMaster Company represented a table to obtain the experience needed for the next table called Global Baseball. He explained that I was transitioning to a new table called ministry to the Jewish people.

I arrived in White Plains in October of 2008. It was a pleasure to be with Terri in our new apartment. I would have a few months before starting school to rest, get to know the area, and spend time with new friends and my family.

The Lord is first in my life, then Terri and the children. I desired to make up to them for all the time away from home getting Global Baseball up and running. All ministry is built upon the foundation of an intimate relationship with the Lord, wife, and children. If I deviate from this foundation it leads to physical and spiritual burnout. I have learned some strong lessons on these core values and they are the most important in my life. You can go off and be used to save the world, but if you do not love the Lord first, then your wife, children, and parents, you have deviated from what is the strength of true ministry. I was looking forward to hanging out more with Terri, Melissa, Joseph, and Benjamin. This move would allow me to invest in my family.

Brethren, my heart's desire and prayer to God for Israel
is that they might be saved.
For I bear them witness that they have zeal for God,
but not according to knowledge.
For they being ignorant of God's righteousness, and seeking to establish
their own righteousness, have not submitted to the righteousness of God.
For Christ is the end of the law for righteousness to everyone who believes.
(Romans 10:1-4 NKJV)

Jeff on the Temple Mount in Jerusalem, Israel

Jeff with Gershon Solomon who desires to rebuild the
Temple In Jerusalem. Gershon is an Israeli war hero and is the
Founder of the Temple Mount Faithful group

Chapter 20:

Walking Through the Storms

In January of 2009, I began my Master of Divinity Degree in Jewish Studies in Manhattan. I began this journey at fifty-four years old. I would end up taking 101 credit hours, which included four classes in Hebrew, and five in Greek. One day in my second class of Hermeneutics, I did not do so well on a quiz. It was only my second class. I went to the director of the seminary. He also taught many of my classes. I expressed my concern about my grades and how I would do.

He put his arm around me and said, "Not to worry; you come to learn and I will worry about the grades."

The same thing happened in Greek II. This was the hardest academic class I ever took. At *God seems to send an angel when I need it.* mid-term I had a C and did not pass my mid-term exam. I was so tired. I had just come off of seventeen speaking engagements in fourteen days and I was out of gas. How am I going to get through school?

So I prayed and said, "Lord, Greek is like math and this was always my weak subject. I am giving it my best effort and I have hit diminishing returns. I am putting this problem in Your hands."

My Greek teacher really knew her Greek. When she came in with my second try on my mid-term, I thought that I was sunk.

A fellow student who was coaching me looked at her and said, "Jeff, knows this material, but he needs more time to memorize the concepts."

My teacher agreed and said that she was going to be my coach and get me through the hard principles. It was incredible. With her help and sticking through the hard spot, I ended up getting a good grade. I also learned that if God has a plan for your life and it looks like you cannot take another step, He will provide and take over. I went on to do well in Greek and actually use it to this day.

About six months after I began seminary, the people who were renting our home in Georgia both lost their jobs and could no longer afford to live in our home. They left our home and took residence elsewhere and I had to carry the mortgage and our rent in New York for a few months. This was difficult. I was a full time student, managed Global Baseball, and had spring, fall, and weekend speaking engagements.

A few weeks later, I was in Villa Rica, Georgia, at the home of Sonny Miller. He had me stay in his uncle's safari house. Before I went to bed, I told Sonny and Karina about a friend, Tony Loefler, who sings like Johnny Cash. One of my favorite songs he sings is, "How Great Thou Art." I also mentioned to them that Terri and her parents are Swedish.

As I was going to bed I noticed that I was humming, "How Great Thou Art," Johnny Cash style, under my breath. As I approached the lamp stand by my bed, I noticed a new hymnal on the lamp stand and turned to the song, "How Great Thou Art," and found it was written by a Swedish pastor. I then sensed the presence of the Lord with me in the room. I laid in bed in the most beautiful presence of the Lord and I prayed.

"Lord, are You in here with me?"

He said to me, "I know about your house and school and all of your concerns. Everything is going to be okay. I have your back. Don't worry; everything is going to be okay."

I went to bed with this in my mind and I thanked the Lord. When I woke up the same special presence was in the room and I read my Bible and said, "Lord, is there anything further You want me to know?"

He told me to go to Sonny and Karina and tell them what happened in the room. So, the next morning I told them about the Lord's visit and that I was singing "How Great Thou Art," found a hymnal by the bed, and how the Lord is greater and bigger that all of our problems. He knows about them and will bring us through the storms of life. As I was speaking with Sonny and Karina, their young daughter turned on the radio, and the song playing was, "How Great Thou Art." We all got goose bumps!

Over the course of the three and a half years that it took me to finish school, the Lord brought new tenants, and Terri and I were able to refinance our home at a better rate and a fifteen-year mortgage.

In May 2012, I graduated from Talbot Theological Seminary of Biola University in La Mirada, California. Terri and I attended the ceremony along with two friends who were also graduating from the program. This was a beautiful school with olive trees and great weather.

When I got to New York, the Lord had me where He wanted me to be and the doors for Global Baseball continued to open. We had a Board of Directors of about twenty members who have all gone with me somewhere worldwide to do a project. My baseball mentor, Brian Doyle, who was the leading hitter in the 1978 World Series, came on board with Global Baseball as our Executive Vice President in charge of Curriculum and Player Development.

Since moving to New York, Global Baseball has done programs in Israel, Cuba, Dominican Republic, Ecuador, Nicaragua, Germany, and Brazil, with new doors opening in Austria, Hungary, and Kosovo. There are now eighty house churches in Cuba and we are training Christian leaders in theology and doctrine throughout the nation. The Cuban government has given us permission to travel and plant churches anywhere on the island of Cuba. They have explained to me that they do not have any problem with us sharing our faith in Jesus; instead they appreciate how we take compassion on their people and the times we have brought humanitarian aid.

After selling our home in Georgia, Terri and I purchased a home in West Nyack, N.Y. and I have been accepted to Nyack Alliance Theological Seminary to work on my Doctoral Degree in Global Leadership. I never imagined that I would ever work on a Doctoral Degree, but the Lord has made this possible. My doctoral project is on evangelism training for the Cuban house church seminary.

As I now reflect on the next steps of my life, I am so grateful for the Lord's redemption of which I am undeserving. I cannot thank the Lord enough for putting special angels along my way to help me. They were the Barnabas people who were able to recognize that God was not done with me. At this juncture of my life, instead of being a Christian leader who leads from the top, I truly want to get underneath the next generation of young Christian leaders. It is my desire to identify the young Joshua's who will take the baton of Global Baseball from me. It is my desire to mentor and equip these young Joshua's who will take GYBF to the next level.

Having then gifts differing according to the grace that is given to us, let us use them: if prophecy, let us prophesy in proportion to our faith; or ministry, let us use it in our ministering; he who teaches, in teaching; he who exhorts, in exhortation; he who gives, with liberality; he who leads, with diligence; he who shows mercy, with cheerfulness.
(Romans 12:6-8 NKJV)

Family picture: Joseph, Terri, Jeff, Melissa, and Benjamin

Picture of Jeff and Terri

Final Reflection

As I take a moment to reflect on my life, I see a few thematic threads. Before knowing Jesus there was an emptiness that things, money, sex, popularity, and position could not fill. When He brought me to Himself and shared His warmth, things began to change. Due to pride and making wrong decisions, I was derailed and almost destroyed myself. The Lord heard my prayers the day I gave my life to Him and He never gave up on me.

He reached down from Heaven and snatched me out of Satan's hands and looked me in the eye and said, "You are My child. I am not done with you!"

I wanted to give up on myself because I was so ashamed of my sin. It was then that I realized what He did on the cross. In Matthew 27:46, when Jesus was on the cross, He cried out to His Father and said, "My God, My God, why have you forsaken me." That was the greatest moment in the history of mankind. It was the moment that all the sins of the world were poured out on Jesus. This was the only moment in which Jesus' relationship with His Father was fractured and He could feel the pain of the separation because of sin. It was at that moment that Jesus took my sin and dealt with it forever. When I realized this, I made a promise to the Lord that I would never again let anyone interfere with my relationship with

Him. If I should fall short due to sin or a moment of deviation from His will, I would ask forgiveness and move on quickly.

It does not pay or satisfy to live for myself. The Lord gave me a burning bush experience. After going through a dark night of correction, the Lord brought me out into the light that I might reflect His light and warmth to others the rest of my days.

The Lord has revealed to me my life's purpose. It continues to unfold every day. I live for Him one day at a time and one person at a time. It is very simple. I just say, "Lord, what would You have me to do today?" If the problems seem too big for me, I pray, "Lord, the problems are too big for me, but not for You. I give them to You and ask for help."

I love the Lord because He has heard my voice and the voice of my supplications. Because He has inclined His ear to me, therefore I will call upon Him as long as I live. The pains of death surrounded me, and the pangs of Sheol laid hold of me. I found trouble and sorrow. Then I called upon the name of the Lord. O Lord, I implore you, deliver my soul! Gracious is the Lord, and righteous. Yes, our God is merciful. The Lord preserves the simple. I was brought low, and He saved me. Return to your rest, O my soul, For the Lord has dealt bountifully with you. For you delivered my soul from death, my eyes from tears and my feet from failing. I will walk before the Lord in the land of the living. What shall I render to the Lord for all His benefits toward me? I will take the cup of salvation, and call upon the name of the Lord. I will pay my vows to the Lord now in the presence of all His people. Lord you have loosed my bonds. I will offer to You a sacrifice of thanksgiving, and will call upon the name of the Lord. (Psalm 116 NKJV)

The Lord has a purpose for your life. You can have a burning bush experience, too! Would you like to ask Jesus into your heart as Lord and Savior? You can ask Him to lead and guide your life. Have you made some decisions you regret in your life? Have you experienced some feelings of hopelessness? Here is the good news. The Lord is not done with you!

Let's pray together!

Dear Jesus, please come into my heart. I believe that You have a plan for my life. I have sinned before You and need Your forgiveness. Please fill me with Your Holy Spirit and give me wisdom on how to live each day. Lord, I realize that You are the judge and can make something beautiful of my life as I turn to You now. Lead me to a good church where I can receive good biblical teaching in a loving environment.

In Jesus' (Yeshua's) name
Amen!

Your brother in Jesus (Yeshua)
Jeffrey (Yoseph) Siegel

About the Author

Jeff Siegel is the founder and President of Global Youth Baseball Federation, Inc. He was born and raised in a Jewish home in Chicago. Jeff came to faith in Jesus as Messiah in 1976 while playing and coaching on the University of Illinois baseball program. This decision made a big impact on his life and family. Jeff has a unique background in both, business management, and professional baseball. In the past, he had a rewarding management career with the ServiceMaster company. Jeff also worked as a professional instructor with the Doyle School of Baseball. For some time, he scouted with the San Diego Padres and was privileged to make many connections in the world of baseball.

Over the years, Jeff developed a burden for young people to find Christ and for their families to be connected with local churches. He had several opportunities to minister through his baseball activities to youth and their families. In 2000, Jeff decided to develop Global Baseball as a 501 (c) (3) nonprofit organization to achieve his desire to share the gospel through baseball. Jeff's personal ministry developed over the years taking him across the globe and eventually others have joined his cause. Now the organization he started is positioned to make a lasting impact among many nations through baseball, softball, and additional sports opportunities.

Jeff earned his Bachelor of Science Degree in Physical Education at University of Illinois and a Master of Arts in Management of Organizations from Southern Wesleyan University. Jeff also graduated with a Master of Divinity Degree at Biola University in Jewish Studies and is presently working on his Doctoral Degree in Global Leadership at Alliance Theological Seminary in Nyack, New York. Jeff ministers locally and internationally. He and his wife Terri live in New York. They have three children, Melissa, Joseph, and Benjamin.

Author Contact Information

Jeff Siegel
678-595-1931
jsiegel@globalbaseball.org
www.globalbaseball.org